D1072184

# Inservice Education for School Administration

D.ep.
LB
2805
A466

# Inservice
# Education
# for
# School
# Administration

*Report of the
AASA Commission
on Inservice Education
for
School Administration*

**American Association of School Administrators** .

= Commission on Inservice...

LB 2805
.A466

COPYRIGHT 1963

AMERICAN ASSOCIATION OF SCHOOL ADMINISTRATORS

1201 Sixteenth Street, N.W.          Washington 6, D.C.

INDIANA-
PURDUE
LIBRARY
WITHDRAWN
FORT WAYNE

*Price: $6*

Library of Congress
Catalog Card Number          63-10143

All rights reserved. No part of this book may be reproduced in any form without permission in writing from the publishers. Order by title and stock number: 021-00486.

# Foreword

It is trite to say, but nevertheless true, that cultural change in this period of history is taking place at an almost breathtaking rate of speed. Everywhere one looks, there is change—rapid change. Community life assumes different characteristics and new dimensions; population growth is phenomenal; people are on the move from rural areas to larger industrial centers and from the central sections of the big cities to the suburbs: suburbia stretches out further and further along arterial highways leading from metropolitan centers in every part of the country; scientific discovery and invention almost outpace the ability of man to comprehend them; old definitions of roles and responsibilities are overtaken by new realities; everywhere men are called upon to reorient long-established images, expectations, principles, and values to new situations; old values are being re-examined and some abandoned without careful public scrutiny; new skills and competencies are needed as school officials wrestle with problems that are unwieldy and difficult to comprehend in their true proportions.

There is scarcely a cultural change or shift in general public policy which does not have its implications for education. School boards, school superintendents, and communities of people again and again are faced with the difficult tasks of reshaping the instructional program; constructing new school plants; finding new sources of school revenue; introducing and using new materials, new methods, and new equipment; changing the boundaries of school districts; and revising patterns of administrative organization. Many of the most perplexing problems that confront them must be faced without precedent or research findings for guidance. New and different solutions to new and old problems must be found.

It was for the purpose of providing assistance to school superintendents and their boards of education in dealing with perplexing problems—both old and new—that the Commission on Inservice Education for School Administration was created by the Executive Committee of the American Association of School Administrators. This commission was charged with the responsibility of projecting, in bold outlines, the conceptions of a program of services that would assist the educational leadership of this country in gaining the insights, in acquiring the information, and in developing the skills needed to deal effectively with the pressing and complex problems of school administration.

As the members of this commission have freely contributed of their time and effort, they have visualized and projected a continuous program of services that would deal with live, vital problems, that would draw

APR 6 1970

upon the disciplines of many fields, that would develop sensitivity to emerging issues, and that would give the depth and breadth of vision essential in planning for the future as well as provide solutions to immediate problems that press for action. They have projected a program of services in which local districts, intermediate districts, state departments of education, colleges and universities, and individual administrators and school board members would be vitally involved. It is to these agencies and to these people, individually and collectively, that this publication is addressed.

The intent of the Commission has not been to lay down the outlines of an inservice program in definitive terms. Rather, it has been to suggest procedures, to identify resources, and to stimulate action programs through which professional assistance and technical information are used to good advantage as superintendents—together with their school boards, teaching staffs, and lay citizens of their school districts—unite their efforts in working out solutions to their own problems. Responsibilities, too, have been boldly identified. This publication suggests courageous steps in the development of the inservice program for school administration which this country needs and must have. To the extent that it fails to encourage state associations of school administrators, institutions of higher education, state educational agencies, and local school districts to take the initiative and responsibility for developing and sustaining a program of services that will enable the school administrators in this country to meet the educational challenges that are now before them and that lie immediately ahead, it will fall short of its purpose.

This document, important as it is, will do little toward making America's schools as good as they ought to be and must be unless the superintendents seize it as an instrument, use it for their own guidance, and share it with others in developing and sustaining the inservice programs they need and want. To the extent that superintendents in intermediate units, in small school systems, and in large cities use it in study with their school boards, with their administrative staffs, with principals, and with teachers will its true value be realized.

FINIS E. ENGLEMAN
Executive Secretary
American Association of
School Administrators

# Acknowledgments

The AASA Commission on Inservice Education for School Administration and, indeed, the entire profession are deeply indebted to the men and women in colleges and universities, state departments of education, state associations of school administrators, and local school systems who have given unsparingly of their time in assisting the Commission with its work. In truth, it may be said that this publication is, in many respects, a reflection of their beliefs, points of view, and experiences. Without their assistance, it would have been impossible to have produced a publication of this nature.

The Commission is especially indebted to Benjamin C. Willis who, as president of the American Association of School Administrators, saw the need for strengthening and improving the services to school administration in this country and took the initiative in appointing the Commission and charging it with the responsibilities it has sought to meet; to Finis E. Engleman for his encouragement, guidance, and support of the Commission's work; to William J. Ellena who prepared the index and critically read the entire manuscript; to Beatrix Sebastian who worked with the Commission from beginning to end and handled the manuscript with painstaking care at every stage in its development; to Janet A. Leban for special editorial assistance; and to the many authors and publishers who have graciously given permission to include excerpts from their published materials in this report of the Commission.

# AASA Commission on Inservice Education for School Administration

RALPH E. CLABAUGH, superintendent of schools, Arlington Heights, Illinois

SHIRLEY COOPER, *chairman*, associate executive secretary, AASA, Washington, D.C.

ZENO B. KATTERLE, dean, College of Education, Washington State University, Pullman, Washington

HOWARD G. NUNN, superintendent, Harper Creek Community Schools, Battle Creek, Michigan

TRUMAN M. PIERCE, dean, School of Education, Auburn University, Auburn, Alabama

WENDELL H. PIERCE, superintendent of schools, Cincinnati, Ohio

WILLIAM J. SANDERS, commissioner of education, State Board of Education, Hartford, Connecticut

T. STANLEY WARBURTON, associate superintendent of schools, Los Angeles, California

THOMAS W. WATKINS, supervising principal, Southern Lehigh School District, Coopersburg, Pennsylvania

# Contents

# Dimensions of the Problem

School administration in the United States—What is it? In the strictest sense of the term, it is the act of administering; it is what school administrators and all who work directly with them do in stimulating, coordinating, and giving direction to the educational enterprise. It is purpose; it is organization; it is a group of people with their leaders at work in a situation where the prevailing social philosophy is democracy and where government is responsive to the will of the people. It is leadership striving to help all people who are affected by school administration understand their roles, feel their responsibilities, and work effectively toward meeting them. "What the administrator does is a vitally important aspect of administration. But what is done correspondingly by the professional staff, the board of education, and members of the community is an equally important aspect of administration."[1]

In a broader sense, school administration is the people in a state or local community exercising their political powers in a free democratic government to shape the institution of public education, to give it character and substance, and to use this instrument of their own creation to serve a common need.

School administration is individuals feeling a responsibility for their schools and doing something about it. It's our next door neighbor; it's the editor of the county paper; it's the cashier in the bank at the corner of Fourth and Main; it's Mrs. VanAshbloom who lives in the big white house at the top of the hill; it's 180 million people working together through their school boards, their legislatures, and their state departments of education to build schoolhouses, hire teachers, and educate the children and youth of this land.

---

[1] Ramseyer, John A., and others. *Factors Affecting Educational Administration: Guideposts for Research and Action.* Columbus: College of Education, The Ohio State University, 1955. p. 2.

1

School administration is 50 state departments of education and 35,000 school districts with all the laws and rules and regulations that guide and direct them. It's 140,000 school board members and what they do in meeting after meeting extending from the late afternoon far into the night; and it's what the school superintendent does in board meetings, in conferences with his staff, and in an address to the downtown Rotary Club at its Wednesday luncheon meeting.

School administration is planning the program of instruction, developing the school budget, levying taxes, and collecting the money needed to operate the schools. It's bonding the property of the school district to build new schoolhouses; it's procuring a school site, designing a school building, and equipping a school library; it's planning courses of study, measuring pupil progress, and establishing standards for graduation; it's finding the best way to teach children to read and to spell and to solve algebraic equations; it's planning evening classes in which adults can become better acquainted with broad social issues about which they must express an opinion at the coming election; and it's discovering safer ways of transporting children to and from school, of handling power-driven equipment in the school shop, and of using chemicals in the laboratory. School administration is what people all over this land do in planning, supporting, and operating the schools.

School administration is leadership that inspires individuals and groups of people to higher purposes and greater efforts and helps them to see their own responsibilities and commitments in broader perspective. Not all the forces that shape the school originate within. The administrator who can lead the staff, the school board, and the people of the community to rise above their daily tasks and see the school with fresh new vision is summoning the energy and marshaling the forces necessary to keep the school vitally alive. School administration is defined by the American Association of School Administrators as "the total of the processes through which appropriate human and material resources are made available and made effective for accomplishing the purposes of an enterprise. It functions through influencing the behavior of persons."[2]

School administration is close to people. It touches parents in such intimate ways as the grade on their little 10-year-old daughter's report card and the time she gets on the school bus in the morning. Most people think of school administration in terms of what is done and what happens

---

[2] American Association of School Administrators. *Staff Relations in School Administration.* Washington, D.C.: the Association, a department of the National Education Association, 1955. p. 17.

in their own districts. But like neighborhoods and communities, towns and cities, and counties and states, no two districts are exactly alike. They differ in size of geographic area and population, in the ethnic and cultural backgrounds of the people, in community customs and traditions, in economic wealth, and in expectations from the schools. And school administration within the districts is as unique as the personality of the superintendent. Anyone who has traveled a bit over the country and studied school administration to any extent can point to an example of almost any kind of school district that can be imagined.

There is a county-unit district in Southern West Virginia with a five-member board, 6 high schools, and 30 grade schools scattered over 800 square miles. Stanley Jeranco has been superintendent in this district for the past 20 years. This is a coal mining county. When the mines are operating at full capacity and everybody is employed, the superintendent and board have found it relatively easy to raise money for the schools. But when the mines are slack and employment drops off, times quickly get hard in this county, and raising the necessary money for teachers and needed equipment becomes difficult. To further accentuate the difficulty of administrative problems, mechanization of the mining industry has thrown many men out of work.

Joe Spivak is the superintendent of Union School District Number 137 in the state of Maine. There are five local school districts and five boards of education in this union. Joe is superintendent of all of them. The first week in every month is a big week for him. Monday, Tuesday, Wednesday, Thursday, and Friday nights—one after the other—he meets with the boards, advising them and giving them assistance wherever possible in shaping the broad outlines of their school programs, in employing instructional staffs, and in purchasing the equipment needed to operate the schools. His task is further complicated by the differences in these districts. One of them, a resort town down on the coast, is flooded with vacationers in the summertime. During these summer months, it is a beehive of activity, with everybody involved in taking care of the tourists. But this little village assumes many of the characteristics of a ghost town during the winter months when the vacationers have left. Another district farther inland is a county-seat town. Here, the population is stable. The work around the courthouse, the meetings held by the board of supervisors, and the meeting of the circuit court at regular intervals give the people of this village a feeling of community pride that is never treated lightly, a feeling that is reflected in their attitude toward the schools.

The Saguaro School District in Southeastern New Mexico, for as long as anyone in the town could remember, had gone peacefully along with its 8 high school teachers and 12 elementary teachers. Nearly all the children in this village and from the homes on the surrounding ranches attended the elementary school. About half of them completed a high school education. But things are different now in the Saguaro School District. A few months ago, the Air Force started building a new airstrip just outside the village limits. Hundreds of workmen and their families have moved into town, and the schools are flooded with new children. The enrollment has increased 200 percent within a month or two. The superintendent and the school board are harassed by problems of finding space and teachers to take care of the children. Furthermore, these newcomers are 'not satisfied with the type of program that has been offered in the schools in past years. Many of the parents are insisting on kindergartens for the very young children and on more mathematics, language, shop, and electronic courses in the secondary schools. The superintendent and the board cannot keep up with the demands made on them, and they do not have money enough to do what they know ought to be done.

Melvin Plotz is the superintendent of a small city district in Southern Wisconsin. The population of this district has not changed very much over the past 20 years, but youngsters of high school age are remaining in school longer, and the time has come when the community must face the problem of constructing a new high school building. This is the one opportunity in a generation that the people of this city will have to build a good school, and they want to do the job well. The board and the superintendent are asking the people to help them think ahead in planning and constructing a building that will be as useful 20 years from now as it is today; that can be readily adapted to new methods of instruction and changes in the curriculum; that students will be proud of and have respect for; and that will be sturdy and durable over the years and yet not cost too much.

Mike Harrigan is superintendent of a newly formed administrative unit in Idaho in which seven rural school districts have been brought together. While the legal steps to combine these seven districts into a single unit have been taken, a school district actually has not yet been created. In questions about the schools, the people continue to think in terms of their own neighborhoods and communities rather than in terms of the total district. They act like an association of seven little districts, each suspicious and jealous of the other. Five successive times, the school board and the superintendent have asked the people to authorize a bond issue to build a new high school, and five times it has been voted down. The children are still attending three small, outmoded high schools that formerly existed and that everybody recognizes as totally inadequate.

Walter Purdy has just been elected to a superintendency in the state of Georgia. For the past 10 years, he has been serving the people of his county as an agricultural extension agent. As he moved over the county advising people about field crops, garden vegetables, and livestock, he became well known. Many people encouraged him to be a candidate for the school superintendency. Walt didn't think much of this for a while because he liked being a county agent. Nevertheless, the idea of becoming the county superintendent intrigued him, and he let his name be put on the ballot. He was pleased and a bit flattered to be elected. But it was a shock to him to realize a week or two after his election that he would be meeting with the school board within the next few months to employ personnel, to purchase school supplies, and to prepare a budget for the whole county school district. Even more frightening was the realization that elementary teachers would be coming to him with questions about teaching beginners to read or about art instruction in the fourth grade.

Louis Burkmeyer is the superintendent of a high school district in the suburbs of a large city. He never openly admits it, but he quietly gets considerable satisfaction from having his associates refer to his as a silk-stocking district. Every one of the five-member board is a college graduate whose annual salary is over $20,000. The board and the school patrons in this district are unwilling to settle for anything less than the very best schools. They want their children prepared for admission to prestige colleges. The superintendent knows that entrance requirements in these schools keep getting tougher and more restrictive year after year. Somehow, he must keep pace with these entrance requirements or convince his board and the people in the school district that the price in terms of pressures and tensions on the young people is becoming too dear to pay.

Tom Swenson is a county superintendent in Nebraska, elected by a vote of the people for a four-year term. There are 60 one-room schools in his county, each with its own school board and its own budget. The average enrollment in the schools is only 12 pupils. Reorganization of school districts and consolidation of attendance areas is the biggest challenge confronting this county superintendent. The people of the county know that reorganization of school districts would bring their children better education; but because the smaller districts enable them to keep school taxes down, they are reluctant to give them up.

Phil Nestor is the superintendent of schools in a Midwestern city with a population of 250,000. This school district has been growing rapidly, and it has been necessary to increase the staff each year, adding specialists in guidance, transportation, business management, food service, audiovisual instruction, health, music, and art. The superintendent has tried to secure the best people for these positions. The prestige of the school district and the relatively high salary schedule have enabled him to get top-flight people. Each new employee has tried to make a reputation for himself by doing his job well. With concentration of effort and growing specialization, school administration is developing into a cluster of bureaus. The program of the school district is splintering into unrelated segments and lacks the coherence and unity it ought to have.

Molly Yamato is the superintendent of an elementary district in Southern California. For the past several years, the teachers in this district have selected a problem around which their inservice growth activities for the year are concentrated. This year, the teachers are giving special attention to the improvement of reading. The school board in the district supports this project. But the teachers were pretty good to begin with, and the superintendent is hard pressed to provide the leadership needed by a highly competent and forward-looking staff.

There is no end to the needs in school administration in this country, and the diversity of circumstances in which the needs exist stretches the imagination. There is Fred Patapsco in a booming new settlement in the Columbia River basin, where there was nothing but sand and sagebrush only a few years ago. Now it is a checkerboard of irrigated farms with families gathered from all parts of the country. There is José Otera in a small school district in the Rio Grande basin where most of the children coming into the classrooms speak only Spanish. The parents of these children are laborers on the fruit and vegetable farms in the district who look forward to the time when the children can be taken out of school to work in the fields and add to the family income. There is Mark Lampliter, superintendent of an Ozark Mountains school district that is losing school population. And there is Newt Sherman, superintendent of schools in a large Northern city that is reeling from the effects of the in-migration of people with few occupational skills, low incomes, and many children.

When we think of public education in this country, we think of communities of people, of school districts, and of school superintendents not wholly unlike the illustrations that have just been given. In this crucial period of history when the institution of public education is put to its severest test, men and women like those briefly described have been called to the strategic leadership position of school superintendent. They serve in both large and small school districts, in cities and towns, and in villages and open-country areas. As the people of this nation seek to make schools better, boards of education look to the superintendent for counsel and advice, faculty members turn to him for leadership, and communities of people rely on his judgment and depend on him for information needed in making decisions. To the extent that he fails, the children in his district are being denied the educational opportunities to which they are entitled.

### Who Can Help?

The dizzying pace of cultural change brings a multiplicity of new problems, ranging from technological invention to a body of new knowledge which is increasing in geometric proportions and is crucial to the culture of the times. Every superintendent is confronted with the need for broader understanding and greater skill as a professional leader. To put it simply and bluntly: If he will do his job well, he must have help. But to need help and to secure help are two entirely different matters. *Traditionally, the people of this country have not lodged with any agency or institution a substantial measure of responsibility for providing inservice assistance to school administration.*

Colleges of education, for the most part, have devoted their energies and their resources to preservice programs. With but few exceptions, these institutions have not been expected to provide more than a nominal service to the school systems in the areas near them. Their budgets have not been planned with such services in view. Staff members with the skill and understanding needed to provide effective service to superintendents, board members, and teaching staffs have not been employed in sufficient numbers. Such limitations stand out clearly when the field service programs in colleges of education are compared to the field service programs of colleges of agriculture, business administration, and engineering.

State departments of education in most states have had neither the resources nor the personnel essential for working effectively with local school systems in inservice programs. Calling attention to such deficiencies is by no means an indictment of state departments of education. Rather, it is simply stating a fact in a manner which calls attention to a leadership function of state departments of education that has not been well recognized or well supported in past years.

Perhaps due to these inadequacies in institutions and governmental agencies, a growing number of consultative firms, operating on a commercial basis, has developed in recent years to provide superintendents and local school districts with such assistance. Undoubtedly, many of these commercial firms are making important contributions to the solution of difficult school problems. One can easily point to school buildings that are constructed better, to curriculum content that is more effectively organized, and to instructional methods that have been improved by such services. But all too often, the fees are so high that only the stronger districts can secure such services. And there are undoubtedly other instances in which such services are provided by people not as well informed about school matters as they should be.

## The Profession Advances

The recent standards set for membership by the American Association of School Administrators go beyond the professional preparation of many men and women who are now employed and doing commendable jobs in school superintendencies. The 1961 amendment to the AASA Constitution provides that, "Beginning on January 1, 1964, all new members of the American Association of School Administrators shall submit evidence of successful completion of two (2) years of graduate study in university programs designed to prepare school administrators and approved by an accreditation body endorsed by the Executive Committee of AASA." While this amendment assures these men and women that they will not be deprived of memberships they already hold in the Association, they do look forward to and are deeply concerned about improving their own professional preparation to the point where it is comparable in quality—if not identical in content—to the standards in the preservice programs toward which the Association has relentlessly and assiduously moved during the last 15 years.

## The Commission's Assignment

It was against a backdrop of these circumstances and the needs which have been suggested rather than described that the American Association of School Administrators, expressing its will through individual communications, through presidents of state associations of school administrators, through Advisory Council members, and finally through its Executive Committee, acting in totality, caused a special Commission on Inservice

Education for School Administration to be created and charged it with the specific responsibility of making a comprehensive study and report on this whole problem. As the Commission addressed itself to the responsibility assigned it, the purposes that clearly emerged were—

1. To create an image of a continuous inservice program that would strengthen and improve school administration wherever it is reached. This program of services should be so conceived, so organized, and so operated that professional growth and increased competency on the part of all people involved, and particularly of the school superintendent, will be a natural and logical outcome.

2. To lay down principles that will be useful as guidelines to school boards, state departments of education, colleges and universities, professional associations of educational leaders, and lay citizens in general in developing, supporting, and operating a continuous inservice program of services to school administration.

3. To show, by illustration and example wherever possible, the resources and personnel that are needed to support and operate the kind of inservice program that is envisioned. The need for resources should be firmly enough defined to serve as a useful guide to people who have responsibility for initiating and planning such programs. At the same time, it should be flexible enough to permit adaptations to unique circumstances.

4. To show the roles that boards of education, colleges and universities, state departments of education, professional associations of educational leaders, and individuals themselves should play in the initiation, development, support, and operation of an inservice program.

5. To develop guidelines to evaluation of an inservice program that will identify strong points as well as weaknesses, that will call attention to accomplishments as well as to places that have been overlooked or neglected, and that will serve as a basis for continuous improvement.

It is toward these ends that the efforts of the AASA Commission on Inservice Education for School Administration have been directed. These are the broad purposes of this publication.

| # Concept of Administration

$T$HE school is the formal institution established by public policy to prepare children and youth in a systematic fashion to adapt and contribute to society. The school reflects the political and moral values of the civilization it serves; the more advanced and sophisticated the society, the more it values individual freedom, diversity, and justice under law. The broader the concept of freedom and the more government comes to serve the ends of men, the greater the necessity for moral education—education that increases intelligent exercise of free choice for more people. Such education is normative. It is concerned with how people *ought* to behave rather than with how people *do* behave. It is directed toward evolving better goals rather than toward maintaining current goals.

The schools are not apart from the public forum; they are in it and of it. They reflect the moral and political values of the society they serve. Educational programs and policy must be developed and justified in light of general public policy. The qualities of statesmanship requisite for the definition and direction of public business at the most comprehensive levels of authority, therefore, are required of those entrusted with the responsibility for school administration.

School administration is the process by which means and ends are marshaled to achieve the evolving purposes of the school. It is considerably more than managing a tutorial system. Since the schools reflect the moral and political values of the society they serve, administration involves the identification and definition of issues of public policy. It involves mobilizing and activating the political leadership potential of all elements that make up the polity—community, state, and nation—to the end of identifying educational, moral, and political aspirations and devising means for progressing toward them.

### The Organization of Authority

The authority or power to administer the schools is not substantive. It is a power that is delegated by the people, through state constitutional and statutory law, to state and local boards of education and to superintendents who, in turn, delegate power to principals and other officers of the school organization. Responsibility for administration focuses, however, upon the executive officer of the board—upon the superintendent. All major decisions and actions channel through him.

## The Board of Education

Boards are vested with responsibility for policy decisions. They perform a function that is legislative rather than executive. Salary schedules, rules for management of the schools, building programs, changes in curriculum, reorganization of staff, and additions to staff all are based upon and guided by policy. But to reach decisions, the board looks to its executive agent and his staff for information and recommendations.

The board is responsible to the public for the condition of the schools and is answerable for the actions of administrators and teachers in working toward the purposes of the schools. The superintendent is depended upon to detect needs for change in policy, to see need for new policy, and to bring the circumstances surrounding them to the attention of the board. The distinction between the board's function and that of the superintendent is quite clear in a well-run school system. "If you had to do a one-gauge appraisal of a school system," the American Association of School Administrators stated in its Thirty-Fourth Yearbook, "you could do worse than to take a barometric reading of its school board-superintendent relationships."[1]

## The Staff

To lead or to accept responsibility for an institution as vital as the public schools, the superintendent must have full and comprehensive knowledge of conditions that prevail at present and some idea of objectives toward which he would move. To gain such understanding, administrators cannot escape responsibility for conducting continuous and vigorous inquiry into the condition of the schools, the district, and the nation. In addition to broad understanding of the issues at stake and the forces at play in the culture of the times, he must have up-to-date

---

[1] American Association of School Administrators. *School Board-Superintendent Relationships*. Thirty-Fourth Yearbook. Washington, D.C.: the Association, a department of the National Education Association, 1956. p. 25.

acquaintance with professional and technical developments in every aspect of education. Whether he serves in a school district with a large staff that is studded with specialists or is the administrative leader in a smaller district where he goes it alone, he will be turned to for counsel, advice, and recommendations for improvement. Ultimate responsibility for every major decision will rest with him. It is necessary that staff decisions be subject to his approval, since his administrative decisions are subject to approval by the board and the board's decisions are, in turn, reviewed and approved or disapproved by the public. Such is the process that time and experience have proven to be effective in keeping the schools responsive to the will of the people and operating under their control.

It is not enough for unit heads, special consultants, or any professional persons who hold responsible positions in the school system to discharge their appointed responsibilities in accord with established policy and decisions clearly bounded by the limits of that policy. Rigid adherence to such practice rapidly leads to mechanical performance that smothers the creative abilities of staff members and saps the vitality of the school. Initiative must be kept alive at every level. A vigorous school system derives a large measure of its strength from the staff's repeatedly meeting and overcoming challenges. There must be a clear and readily accessible way for them to have impact upon administrative action at a higher echelon and upon policy decisions at the highest level. In an administrative climate where such flow of ideas and opinions is discouraged or prevented, the full potential of the staff is not in use, and preparation for positions of higher responsibility is neglected. Yet, a well-run school system is not a debating society. The superintendent cannot evade his responsibility to exercise judgment or allow decisions to be made by others that should be made by him.

*Leadership Function*

Leadership on the part of the board and the superintendent, as well as in the lower echelons of administration, is strong and inspiring to the extent that the relationship described above is maintained in decision making. Mutual respect is engendered and confidence is maintained when there is clearly defined procedure for communication of facts, opinions, and ideas needed for sound judgment. Deliberation on the merits of a plan of action can be carried on in the system from several points of view. If this is done, it probably will become a better plan and, when put to the test, it will have enough built-in support for a fair trial.

Furthermore, a strong unifying element is added to the system: The leadership function of the board is strengthened because its policies have been well conceived and well carried out, and the public rallies to its support; the leadership of principals is strengthened because the teachers have been involved beyond the point of mere consultation—they have had a part in the initiation of a plan of action and a part in the deliberations that led to the decision; and the leadership of the superintendent comes to fruition in a smoothly functioning organization moving toward its purpose.

. . . the true test of an administrator may be, not his ability to design and respect organization charts, not his ability to keep within channels, but his ability to concert and release the energies of men for the attainment of public objectives. It might be argued that the essence of successful administration is: first, to acquire the ideas and information necessary for wise decisions; second, to maintain control over the actual making of the decisions; and, third, to mobilize men and women who can make the first two things possible—that is, who can provide effective ideas and information, and who can reliably put decisions into effect. It is conceivable that these things may be more important than preserving the chastity of administrative organization—that, indeed, an excessive insistence on the sacredness of channels and charts is likely to end in the stifling of imagination, the choking of vitality, and the deadening of creativity.[2]

There is more to decision making, however, than intellectual judgment. A decision is also a moral choice. Conviction without the courage of the conviction is worthless. There must be a strong drive to follow the chosen course of action, as indeed there must have been a strong drive to make a choice in the first place, particularly if the leader did not receive as much support as he had hoped for. If he has every reason to believe he is right, he must be courageous enough to take a stand and hold fast until support comes to him. There is no place in leadership for the pusillanimous. It is a lack of moral power to make decisions and to follow them through to the end rather than a deficiency in intelligence or a defect in intellectual training that causes administrators to fail.

## The Public

Nor is there any chance of success for leadership that is not magnanimous; it must be open minded and large minded. As indicated above, the people, by law, delegate power to boards of education to run the schools. But the people are not done with the problem of educating their children when they have selected representatives to the board.

[2] Schlesinger, Arthur M., Jr. *The Coming of the New Deal.* Boston: Houghton Mifflin Co., 1959. p. 522.

Their interests and concerns become a basis for planning and policy formation. They want schools that are good, and they want schools that are economically managed. They want schools that will develop children to their full capacities. Organized labor is and has been a potent force for the improvement and extension of public education. Industrial and commercial management, to keep abreast of rapid technological changes that bring about accelerated obsolescence of skills, wants an educational program that will lead to greater adaptability of the personnel it employs. Civic as well as industrial leaders want schools that will attract people to the community who will contribute to its civic and economic prosperity. One of the first questions asked prospective employers who are competing for skilled personnel is about the quality of the local public schools.

In arriving at decisions, school leadership must not set itself apart and hide behind a curtain of professionalism. Quite to the contrary, it must devise and sustain means through which the public is kept informed and through which the desires of the public can have impact upon the educational effort. Citizens concerned with civil rights, social welfare, delinquency, and better government represent a vast resource of intelligence and leadership potential. When developed, coordinated, and evolved by local school administration through conferences, *ad hoc* committees, and councils, this potential adds power and zest to community education like a lusty wind in a full-set sail and brings a forward movement in the program that is otherwise impossible.

Such use of the leadership potential residing in the public is essential to preclude administrative oversights and blunders and the subsequent temptation to special-interest groups to move into the void or troubled area with schemes that may well be detrimental to the schools. Examples of such action abound. Their disrupting effects have created a halting and uncertain imbalance in some areas of public education. The great task of administration is to unify the forces of community life and bring these powers to bear in constructive fashion in shaping the educational program.

The various elements of the power structure should not be played off one against another, nor should timidness, fearfulness, or pettiness of mind cause any one of them to be feared, catered to, or avoided. All must be confidently and forthrightly asked to share a responsibility which is, after all, their own. Where administration is successful in achieving such unity in action, a rich, well-balanced, and vigorously developing educational program becomes a reality. Public education is too complex, too expensive, and far too important to have leadership potential needlessly expended in petty bickering or exhausted in unnecessary strife between opposing elements. Public education is so all-important that the task of leadership in operation and support should be carried forward by all in an orderly and a responsible manner.

### Administration—School, Public, Business

Frequently, school administration is compared with public administration and with business administration. There are some elements common to all three, but there are other elements that distinguish school administration from other types of administration.

### Business Administration

A private business organization has three functions: ownership policy making, management, and production. In a corporation, policy is made by a board of directors who represent the stockholders. A small company may be owner-managed, but a large company is managed by a skillful business administrator selected by the board. Production is carried on in the plant. A business enterprise is conducted for the purpose of making a profit for the owner. It is considered to be successful as long as it makes a profit, and fails when it continues to operate at a loss. Its objective, therefore, is specific and clear, and so is the measure of its success. There is no question about the motivation of the directors, who are chosen because of their knowledge and skill in guiding the policy of this particular organization. There is no question about the abilities required of management, nor is there any question about proving the competence of management. Failure to produce profits results in change of management.

### Public Administration

An organization that carries on public business has the same three functions, but its purpose is to provide services to the public. It is not run for profit, but for the common good, a purpose much more difficult to define. It is the people who determine what is to be done and how much money is to be spent doing it. Policy is determined by their representatives. But the people and their representatives speak with many voices, and opinions as to what is needed and how much should be spent are varied and opposed. Diversity in public interest and intent is resolved and translated into policy through political action. The representatives of the people who are making policy decisions are at the same time making political decisions; they are practicing what is commonly called "the art of the possible."

The directors of public policy chosen by the people are not necessarily chosen for their knowledge of public affairs or their skill in guiding the conduct of the public business, although they may do well at it. For the most part, they come into office through political channels and are responsive to the will of the people. Their powers as public administrators are limited not only by political policy, but by legal restraints exerted by statutes and ordinances and their interpretation by higher administrative authorities and by the courts. While administrative procedures and the conduct of public business may be every bit as efficient as the management and conduct of private business, the manager of the public enterprise faces problems quite different from the problems faced by his counterpart in business.

*School Administration*

School administration is a special form of public administration. Education is a state function. Local school boards are creatures of state legislatures; they are agents of the states, not of town or county governments. As such, authority is delegated to them to make policies, such as those governing teacher certification, within the framework of the Constitution and statutes as well as within the limits of regulations established by the state education agency. Some laws are mandatory, some are permissive, and there are some areas of school administration in which the law is silent. Consequently, there are some aspects of school administration where policies must comply, others where the board may or may not adopt policies, and still others where the board is rather free to make policies as long as they are not in conflict with general law. Boards, therefore, generally have considerable freedom, but there is some variation. In some states, they have wider discretionary powers than in others.

The members of school boards are local citizens, but, whether they are appointed or elected, they are not necessarily chosen because of their skill in management, knowledge of law, or understanding of the intricate processes of education. Rather, they are chosen for qualities that appeal to the appointing authority or to the electorate. School boards represent the aspirations of the people they serve. A conscientious board serves as a chamber into which the forces, interests, and desires from community life are continuously funneled, analyzed, and synthesized through political action to the end of better schooling. The board interprets the school program to the community and attempts to rally support for the policies it has adopted.

The school board chooses as its chief executive officer a superintendent who may be compared to executives in business and public agencies. Like them, he has had previous experience in his line of work and has had some formal education designed to prepare him for the position. As a teacher, he is a member of a profession in which there is a unique body of learning and an art that can be acquired, practiced, and communicated. It may be asked whether school administration is, in and of itself, a profession. If it is not, it is close to becoming one. Administrators themselves, with strong support from the general public, have taken the initiative in recent years in such movements toward professionalization of the school superintendency as the following:

... (1) A shift in attitudes and values pertaining to a social function so that the function becomes the target of efforts toward improvement of standards on the part of the leaders identified with the function; (2) the formation of organizations for this purpose on the part of those identified with the function; (3) the development of programs of research activity; (4) the development of institutions for training of personnel; (5) the formulations of standards and codes of practice, including ethical and service criteria; (6) movements toward legal recognition of these standards (licensing, tests, special prerogatives); and (7) the emergence of special terminologies associated with the developing special bodies of knowledge, competence, or values being cultivated.[3]

Institutions of higher learning have designed programs that purport to prepare executives for the fields of education, business, and public administration. Opportunities in the lower levels of management in these fields have been opened to graduates of these institutions, and institutes in management are more commonly being conducted for men and women employed at higher levels of management. Skill and knowledge are required in the management of some enterprises that call for mastery of highly technical information.

The school superintendent must have a general knowledge of education. State certification requirements for the superintendency not only require specialized postgraduate training but also successful experience over a period of time as a teacher and supervisor or administrator at lower levels. The existence of such requirements is evidence that even though local boards may not recognize the need for such training and experience, school administration is recognized, by practice and regulation, as a specialized branch of management that requires a body of

[3] Belisle, Eugene L., and Sargent, Cyril G. "The Concept of Administration." *Administrative Behavior in Education.* (Edited by Roald F. Campbell and Russell T. Gregg.) New York: Harper & Brothers, 1957. p. 96.

theoretical and practical learning and that is coming more and more to be regarded as a profession.

## The Educational Enterprise

The enterprise the school superintendent manages is the complex school system in which the potential of every child from the severely handicapped—mentally, physically, and emotionally—to the academically talented and the artistically gifted is expected to be developed during a period of 12 or 13 formative years. The product of the school is not standardized, nor are its characteristics more than generally predictable. Although basic learnings common and necessary to the humanity of all children are at the core of the program, diversity of abilities is recognized, and variations in interest are encouraged. Even though children are taught in groups, learning is an individual process. There is neither intention nor possibility of restricting the individual personality to a common mold. The very essence of democracy is respect for individual personality. The very strength of America resides in the diverse interests and abilities of its people.

The schools are staffed by specialists who, for the most part, are not interchangeable with each other. There are teachers of art, music, academic subjects, and vocational subjects, the latter designed to prepare pupils for business and industry; there are teachers who are prepared for the primary grades and others who have had special preparation for the intermediate grades; there are teachers of the handicapped, library teachers, school social workers, school psychologists, and guidance counselors; there are supervisors and consultants for special areas; there are principals; and there are personnel responsible for business matters, the physical plant, transportation, and school cafeteria service. The difference between a large system and a small one is in the number of personnel employed, not in the number and variety of special services that are required and that must in some manner be made available.

The administrator, in accordance with policies established by the board, is responsible for finding and employing these experts and for maintaining conditions in which their capabilities can be used to best advantage. He must group them and give them assignments in an organization that operates in a physical plant adequately equipped and supplied, and he must guide them in their work with children in the wide variety of developmental activities required to achieve the purpose of education. Furthermore, he must strive to establish and maintain a climate that fosters improvement. New methods of organization and new techniques must be considered, tried out, and refined to the end of stimulating professional growth of employees and making the schools better at every possible point so that the products of the schools will continue to grow and meet new situations with confidence and skill throughout the life that follows school.

## The Patrons

The patrons of the school are the parents in particular and the public in general. Because of the success of their own schooling and the beneficent effects of the American economy, parents and the general public are becoming better educated and more prosperous; and they are, in turn, hopeful that the younger generation will have even better opportunities than they themselves had. More and more articulate, the impact they make upon the schools through the press and through citizens committees and parents organizations is of ever-increasing importance. The administrator must coordinate into a pattern for the continuing betterment of the school the expectations of the articulate public, the potentialities of the staff, and the results of research that affect the learning process. He must overcome indifference in the staff and, working with the board, he must stir and stimulate interest in segments of community life where there is apathy.

He must stand firm against pressures, whatever their source, that lead to imbalance, to overemphasis of pet ideas, and to innovations that might cause some pupils to flourish at the expense of others or that might result in waste of the time and effort of employees and material resources of the school district. He should not be engulfed by bursts of enthusiasm for untested schemes or for techniques that may be nothing more than fads. Relying on his professional judgment and supported by the wisdom of the staff and a well-informed school board, he must maintain the integrity of the school as an educational institution and defend it against forces that would make it a welfare agency or an indoctrination center used by individuals or groups whose objectives are limited and restrictive rather than conducive to rational growth. The children enrolled in the schools are, in a large measure, in his trust. He cannot allow them to be delivered as a captive audience to any special-interest group.

## Determining Efficiency

The manager of a business enterprise is considered to be successful if the firm makes a satisfactory profit. The manager of a public agency is successful if the agency provides efficient service at reasonable cost.

But the success of a school administrator is not so easily measured. The school makes no profit, and its expenses continue to grow in an aggravating manner because of increase in the number of children served and growing demands from the public. Its most important accomplishments often cannot be observed at once. "Many seeds planted in the hearts and minds of children during their early formative years do not come to fruition immediately. Appraising such fundamental changes in the lives of children cannot be made over a week end as can the taking of an inventory in a hardware store."[4]

Measuring the school's efficiency with a high degree of exactness is difficult. General observations may reveal that more and better-prepared guidance counselors, more clerical help, a smaller pupil-teacher ratio, and more books in the library will result in better schooling. But how much better? It may be held that expenditures for schools in culturally disadvantaged areas should be greater than expenditures for schools in culturally favored neighborhoods. But just how much more is needed to do the job? It is generally agreed that schools will be better if teachers are better prepared and better paid. But, again, the question is this: How much better will they be and how much more should they be paid?

Furthermore, it is not easy to tell whether or not a superintendent is doing a good job. An inept superintendent may move from position to position with the schools in each succeeding district—each position better than the last—for a long period of time without his competence being clearly demonstrated. It is so hard to be sure. The schools grow, and the need for experienced leaders increases. Experience, even if it is not outstanding, may in itself obscure lack of power or quality in administrative leadership. A superintendent may coast along for years, riding on recognition of some past accomplishment or on the coattails of others, without contributing anything worthy of the name of leadership to the school district in which he is employed. On the other hand, a capable superintendent may be underestimated or fall into ill repute because the true worth of what he has accomplished or is trying to accomplish is not recognized or understood, or because the circumstances in which he works are so complex. In either case, sound judgments are hard to make because of the lack of instruments for measuring the accomplishments of the school and the true quality of performance by the administrator and his staff.

---

[4] American Association of School Administrators. *Judging Schools with Wisdom.* Washington, D.C.: the Association, a department of the National Education Association, 1959. p. 4.

Business and industry have developed systems of quality control and cost accounting and indexes by which their product can be judged. Because of its different nature, attempts to use these measures for judging the quality and effectiveness of school administration have not met with much success. Nevertheless, it is essential that objective and dependable standards be developed for measuring the quality of schooling—measures that will pinpoint weaknesses in the staff, weaknesses in administration, weaknesses due to unwarranted interference on the part of the board or local government, and weaknesses due to apathy or dissension in the community. Because of the nature of the educational enterprise, it is as important to measure what is put into the school as it is to measure and form judgments about what the school produces. Despite this need, there seems to be not only professional resistance but also public resistance to the development of a thoroughgoing approach to evaluation.

Sentiment based on local pride and nostalgia, as well as on status seeking, affects public attitude. Changes in organization and drastic changes in program meet resistance. The staff, jealous of its prerogatives as a profession, suspects evaluation because it is based upon the judgments of supervisors and administrators who do not inspire confidence. Teachers believe such evaluation to be restrictive and unfair. Because there are so many ways to help children learn and grow, teachers fear the limitation that could be imposed upon teaching by rigorous application of formal methods of evaluation. Teaching procedures, it is feared, might become standardized as routine operations that would discourage professional initiative and experimentation and transform teaching into a mechanical performance. As the professional preparation of staff members increases, there is increased demand for respect for individual judgment.

There are at least two anomalies in this situation. One is that the professional employee is seeking to exercise individual judgment about the quality of performance and the results of an organized, publicly supported enterprise controlled and guided by public policies and dependent upon public acceptance. It is true that in the private professional enterprise, the profession maintains the right to judge its own practices. But practice in the private profession is not nearly as responsive to public controls as are the schools. There is an independence in private professional practice that the schools do not have. The other anomaly is the tacit acceptance of the principle that the judgment of all teachers is equal. This principle is implicit in the single salary schedule, differentiating as it does only on the basis of course credits or degrees and length of service. Classification of employees according to duties performed, as is commonly done in industry and in civil service, is not practiced in the teaching profession.

It is good that teachers be protected from the vagaries of politics by laws governing their employment and dismissal. There is, however, a serious question about the restriction upon administrative judgment exerted by policies and regulations generated by the profession and adopted generally by boards. This problem area of personnel management may underscore more graphically than anything else the urgent need for improving the preparation and selection procedures of school administrators so they will have a greater measure of the confidence of the profession as well as of the public. If school administration is to get better, the methods and implements for measuring the quality of the school and the quality of the staff must be strengthened.

### The Basis of a Theory of School Administration

A sound concept of school administration must be founded upon a sound concept of public education. Public education is growing so rapidly, is so beset by pressures and problems, includes so many areas of specialization, is discussed by so many spokesmen—in short, has become so broad, so varied, and so comprehensive—that neither the public nor the teaching profession can readily and completely comprehend it in its full detail. If professional education in general and school administration in particular are to be respected as disciplines to be learned and practiced, it is time that there be drastic re-evaluation and reorganization of the knowledge and experience held to be essential to this discipline. The content belonging to this discipline should be clearly identified, organized, and brought together in a logical manner rather than allowed to exist as an accretion of descriptive material and opinion. Elementary chemistry at the college level is now taught as physical chemistry. This vast science can now only be held together and communicated by mathematical logic; chemistry has outgrown the descriptive approach of yesterday. A logic or dialectic is also necessary to hold together and communicate what is known about the art of education. This is particularly necessary for the administrator of whom so much general knowledge and wisdom is required.

There are school superintendents who are universally esteemed. They have been instrumental in bringing together staffs of high-quality professional people. The educational program in each of these school districts is well supported through the power structure of community life and is well recognized for its excellence outside the district's boundaries. It has that extra 5 percent that makes the difference between what is ordinary and what is excellent. It is out in front—a step or two ahead of neighboring school districts in coming to grips with vital educational issues. There is a vitality in administration in these districts which makes everyone else in and about the schools enthusiastic about what is being done. The citizens in these districts are proud of their schools' reputations.

What is the source of this exceptional, dynamic power that permeates every facet of administration? Careful observation of these situations strongly indicates that much of this vitality comes from the superintendents themselves. Such men apparently are guided by some rationale. They are lucid, candid, and convincing in their explanation of program. They are bold in their thinking and planning; they are approachable, having established orderly channels through which they may be reached and by which they may reach the representative public. They inspire confidence because they are imbued with confidence in themselves that comes from successful application of the knowledge and skills of their profession. From successful experience as teachers and administrators and careful study of the literature in the field, they know education thoroughly. They know their business and keep themselves thoroughly informed about the system for which they are so largely responsible. Their understanding of the theory of management has not come wholly from information vicariously acquired; rather, it is a blending of philosophical concepts with understanding that has come from vital experiences in working with pupils and teachers and parents in the schools. In Lucien Price's dialogues with Whitehead, near the close of this philosopher's distinguished career, he inquired, ". . . as between your life as scholar and your life as executive, which developed you more?" Whitehead replied:

> I learned my profession out of books, of course; but the administrative work developed me quite as much; in fact, I should be inclined to say, more. But for the continual meeting and dealing and talking with people, I might have stuck in the ruts of an academic scholar.
>
> My own life of action . . . now I come to think of it, goes back to my days as a schoolboy. I was a leader in games, and, though you might not guess it now, a good football player and a passable cricketer. Sherborne was a school of about four hundred boys, ninety of whom lived in the dormitory. As head boy of the school and captain of the playing teams, I had to keep order in the dormitory. So all my life I have had the discipline of having to run things.[5]

---

[5] Price, Lucien. *Dialogues of Alfred North Whitehead.* Boston: Little, Brown and Co., 1954. pp. 245-46.

The true professional in any field of endeavor makes the most difficult task look easy because he has thoroughly mastered the disciplines of his profession or occupation. Guided by a body of philosophical principles and a core of values logically related to each other to which he turns again and again when problems confront him, the professional administrator moves with sureness and confidence. Such blending of practical experience with disciplined study is reflected in the comments of Whitehead, a man who, although he devoted a large part of his life to highly disciplined study in the fields of mathematics and science and had acquired an almost unsurpassed comprehension of the philosophies of the ages, looked upon his practical experiences in working with people as being equally significant in developing his executive abilities.

Wherever we see an outstanding educational program, we see a superintendent who has an abiding commitment to the high purposes of education in a democracy; who has a deep sense of responsibility for the institution of public education; and who knows that the schools are forever being shaped by the decisions and actions of the school board, the staff, children and youth in the classrooms, and citizens in all walks of community life. We see a superintendent with an unfaltering faith in the goodness of people, a superintendent who adheres to a body of principles which guide him in foul and fair weather alike, a superintendent with clearly defined purposes in mind toward which he relentlessly moves and seeks to have the entire school system move with sureness and full confidence. We see a superintendent who is sensitive to the stream of cultural change with its tides which buffet and beat upon the institution of public education, gradually giving it form and character and shaping it to the unquestionable facts of reality.

Sensitive to these forces, the superintendent skillfully directs them—whether they reside in political parties, labor organizations, business enterprise, or in petty feuding between suburbanites and the selfish interests of the "400" living in the more exclusive areas of the district—so their energies and their over-all effects are constructive rather than destructive.

Such ability in practice is guided by a logic that brings together and holds together seemingly disunifying concepts into a dynamic, differentiated whole. Such logic does not have to be learned from firsthand experience or developed through trial-and-error methods. It is a philosophy of education that is concerned with the resolution of such important instructional issues as subject matter versus method, play versus work, interest versus discipline, theoretical study versus practical work experience, science versus the humanities, and practical arts versus fine arts.

The dialectics for the theory of administration should be concerned with issues that arise between educational and fiscal authorities in government, in the working relationships between teachers on the one hand and administration on the other, between local-state and federal support and control, and between the development of general public policies and educational policy as it affects the general public well-being.

# CHAPTER THREE

# Imperatives of Change

$\mathbf{M}$EN and women with broad knowledge and a ready capacity for independent thinking constitute the lifestream of American education today, and are needed in ever-increasing numbers. Though characterized by many qualities, these educational leaders are known chiefly for their ability to think creatively and independently. In thinking for themselves, they are not afraid to pursue unusual as well as tried-and-tested ideas. They work for the solution of perplexing educational problems—those having long-range relevance as well as those that pertain to more immediate needs. Out of these rigorous intellectual pursuits come satisfactions from meeting a challenge and accomplishing some worthy purpose.

Coupled with the school administrator's independent thinking is full realization that, in the solution of persistent and perplexing educational problems, effective action is achieved by working with and through people. This is a process which requires broad, general knowledge, keen understanding of human nature, insight into and tolerance for human frailties, objectivity and fairness of mind, and a clarity in thought that often goes beyond ordinary knowledge of the field of education and of today's social forces. The administrator who is a creative educational leader is a thorough and careful student of the main currents of life around him.

The worth of the educated mind is emphasized by Gilbert Chapman, when he states:

The future security of this country and world rests upon the ability of our educational system to develop the highly educated man. Well-balanced maturity, which is essential to our society, must emanate from the universities. We shall need well-trained and analytical minds that can appraise the problems that surround them. In the days ahead, which will be full of international tension and great economic challenge, the moral and spiritual strength which comes with the educated mind will be essential to the preservation of society.[1]

The full import of education in perpetuating our way of life and the effect of educational leadership upon the educational program are factors of central concern in administration. Administrators, as individuals and as leaders, must be cognizant of the moral responsibilities which rest upon their actions. The significance of the moral hazards of executive decision making is clearly indicated in a challenging manner by Louis William Norris:

For an executive, the chief crises are moral. Since his job is so rarely impersonal, his principal problems are what he does about people. He may have started out as a master craftsman, teacher, or production expert, but as an executive he is daily putting into action plans for people to carry out, which will in turn affect other people. The criteria that guide his actions—his morals in short—are, therefore, the most important features of his term of service as an executive. He is continuously on the radarscope of public judgment . . . one of the key tests is his capacity to face the hazards and problems of:

1. Living with necessity of compromise—but never compromising too much.
2. Being free to disclose only parts of the truth on many occasions, yet needing to see the whole truth.
3. Having to make final decisions but on incomplete facts.
4. Accepting responsibility for the mistakes of subordinates while not allowing them to make too many mistakes.
5. Living up to the image that the public and his associates demand of a man in high office but not becoming the victim of it.
6. Succeeding as a man of thought as well as a man of action.[2]

It is easy to forget, in day-to-day work, the broad imperatives of leadership and the moral forces impinging upon it. The hustle and bustle of a multitude of decisions to be made leaves scant time for necessary introspection. Yet, it is upon the breadth and depth of comprehension of the moral imperatives of decision making—upon understanding and respecting the true magnitude and significance of what administrators do or do not do—that the effectiveness of educational leadership depends.

The social forces of our time that affect how people live and what they do in such dramatic fashion insistently demand correlative changes in the educational program. To guide these changes so they are made to best advantage and so that what needs to be done is done requires

[1] Chapman, Gilbert. *Toward the Liberally Educated Executive.* New York: Mentor Books, 1960. p. 9.

[2] Norris, Louis William. "Moral Hazards of an Executive." *Harvard Business Review* 38: 72; September-October 1960.

educational leadership of the highest order. The educational program that has served our country well for the past 50 years is rapidly being replaced by new content, changing concepts, more diversified curricular offerings, and improved techniques and skills. These must be implemented by concurrent changes in administrative organization, buildings and facilities, and, most important of all, by more highly skilled and resourceful personnel. To bring about the changes needed in orderly process is a problem of far-reaching significance and consequence in school administration.

These demands upon educational leadership place a premium upon broad knowledge, creative thinking, the capacity for working with and through people to accomplish desired results, adaptability and preparedness for change, resourcefulness and a will to do, and, most of all, a true sense of humility. Where personal limitations impede effective action, there must be firm determination to compensate for these shortcomings. The successful school administrator matches skills on equal footing and holds his own with the best leadership in the community. This he does by persuading—not pushing; by leading—not outstripping; by skillfully drawing forth the powers of the people on his staff; and by utilizing the full resources of the community.

### Decentralized Administration Requires a Broad
### Base of Educational Statesmanship

The American system of decentralization in educational administration is currently being put to a severe test. But with full recognition of the severity of this test, the AASA Commission on Inservice Education for School Administration does not advocate centralization of control and management of the schools such as is found in almost every other nation of the world. There is much reason for believing that America's progress in public education may be due in great part to widely decentralized control, to placing the responsibility for education in the hands of people in literally thousands of neighborhoods and communities, to a diffusion of policy making to a degree that amazes and perplexes the European observer of the American educational scene.

Nevertheless, all who share intelligently in controlling the schools and in giving direction to the educational program must be informed of the issues at stake. This may well be thought of as item number one in the current test of decentralized control of education. To the degree that policy is formed by the many and the broad purposes of education determined by the many, to that extent must the many be informed and aware of the import of the responsibilities they carry. By the same token, promising practices, improved administrative procedures, and pertinent research will aid only in those districts where people concerned with school administration, be they laymen or professional educators, are thoroughly familiar with them.

Parochialism of thought in educational matters is more or less a result of local control. When administrators or other educational leaders, due to lack of varied experience or broad perspective, view the schools in their own district as the universe of education in miniature, hopes are dimmed and urges to do something better are stilled by the growing belief that "what is must be." At the risk of oversimplifying the problem, it seems logical to suggest that the direction of the educational enterprise in a modern society must be turned over to a considerably reduced number of thoughtful persons who discern the issues to be resolved *or* that the thousands of administrators who make relatively final decisions about the control and operation of the schools become, each in their own right, educational statesmen of some parts.

Educational administration in America has long been vulnerable to the charge that leaders cannot make up their minds. The "phonics" advocates berate the "sight reading" disciples and vice versa; diversity in the educational program is ridiculed by proponents of basic education; flexible standards of accomplishment are viewed with scorn and disdain by academicians; educators who are presumed to be reputable decry the shortcomings of their colleagues; and countless saviors rush to the fore with devices which they believe to be shortcuts to Utopia. Meanwhile, in countless local school districts, administrators and their staffs and boards of education proceed pretty much on the basis of business as usual. What we need, according to The Fund for the Advancement of Education, in its 1961 Report, are ". . . ways to bring all sound new ideas and techniques together to achieve not just a patchwork of improvement, but a coherent design of advancement."[3] The preparation and perfection of the blueprint for this "coherent design of advancement" might well serve as the goal of those concerned with inservice education for school administration.

### Educational Administration Must Enlarge Its Vision

In every developing nation in the world, educational reform or improvement is becoming a matter of national policy. With a heavy

---

[3] The Fund for the Advancement of Education. *Decade of Experiment.* New York: the Fund, 1961. p. 105.

commitment to the development of the individual, American society has given high priority to education in community life and in state government, but has embraced with some reluctance the concept of education as a crucial element in national policy. Educational administration, devoted as it is to local control and to resistance to state and federal control, often appears to be confused and uncertain. The challenge to school administration in America is to break out of the restrictions that limit leadership so largely to rearranging local educational programs without freezing the ferment and stilling the initiative that has bubbled in neighborhoods and communities throughout the nation as the schools have operated under local control. School administration must meet its full commitment to the nation as a whole without sacrificing its commitment to the community school and the proven values of lay and professional cooperation and planning at the grass roots level.

Dean Francis Keppel of Harvard University, in the first of the Alfred D. Simpson lectures, stated: "By deciding, perhaps wisely, that education on the local and state level should be kept free from political party alignments, school administration on the national scene has lost touch with the forces that initiate and control social reform."[4] He went on to say that one of the central problems facing school administration is the tendency to rely on current public opinion rather than long-term solutions to public issues and that, in his judgment, this country has paid a heavy price for the separation of public administration from school administration.

That each local school system can raise itself to excellence by its bootstraps is a delusion America can no longer afford. The nation cannot fully depend upon the kind of educational program each local community is able to or willing to provide. This is not to say that the direction of the educational enterprise should be taken from the thousands of more or less independent and devoted administrative staffs and local boards and placed with a central educational bureaucracy with headquarters in the state or national capital. This is, however, to suggest that practicing school administrators must somehow convince themselves and the American people that educational leaders should coordinate their efforts and improve their understanding of crucial educational problems and issues through a broadly conceived program of education that involves them and serves them concurrently with the performance of their administrative tasks. "However strongly we

---

[4] Keppel, Francis. *Public Policy and School Administration.* Cambridge, Mass.: New School Development Council, 1961. p. 12.

may believe that public education in America is still entirely a local matter," says President John H. Fischer of Columbia University's Teachers College, "the facts will not support our faith, nor is there any likelihood that a nation whose regional differences diminish every year can meet its educational problems by ignoring common national needs."[5]

A well-planned, carefully implemented, and adequately financed program of inservice education for *all* school administrators would undoubtedly improve and strengthen the quality of education in every school district and would lead to more efficient use of educational manpower. The Commission believes that institutions of higher learning, professional organizations of school administrators, state departments of education, and other appropriate agencies must act promptly and constructively to fill this vacuum if public education in America is to meet its responsibilities. Present spotty and sporadic efforts, good as some of them have been, have not done the job. What is desperately needed is mobilization of the considerable resources in educational research and leadership on a scale and according to a pattern which will make opportunities for professional growth available to *all* school administration in *every* district. Such a program could lead to the breakthrough in educational planning for which today's world so desperately calls.

### Administrators Cannot Work Long on Hoarded Intellectual Capital

The demands now being made upon schools in this period of rapid cultural transition and upon the school administrators who are so largely responsible for the schools make it impractical to place full dependence upon preservice preparation programs and upon the independent initiative of the individual superintendent to keep apace with the demands for leadership placed upon him. Hollis A. Moore, Jr., writing in *Studies in School Administration* in 1957, said:

Important as improvements in pre-service training programs may be, they affect the future much more than the present. Most of the jobs in school administration for the next ten years will almost certainly be held by people who are now school administrators and who have for the most part completed their formal collegiate training. If, then, we are learning from CPEA important new concepts and practices which will improve the performance of school administration, there must be found some way to bring this to the direct attention of school administrators now on the job.[6]

---

[5] Fischer, John H. "Standards for Noah's Ark?" *Time,* March 16, 1962. p. 50.

[6] Moore, Hollis A., Jr. *Studies in School Administration.* Washington, D.C.: American Association of School Administrators, a department of the National Education Association, 1957. p. 96.

Inservice education is by no means a new concept in school administration. The professional growth of teachers is recognized and rewarded by most boards of education. Advances on teachers' salary schedules usually take into consideration additional training after service has begun. Such financial rewards are made on the basis of the widely accepted belief that inservice growth improves the teachers' contributions to the school system and makes for better performance in the classroom. Workshops and inservice programs, at least at the local level, are not unusual in thousands of school systems. That many inservice programs in local school districts for teachers and other personnel are not more fruitful may be due to the fact that the school administrators themselves have not had sufficient opportunity to raise their own sights. In spite of valiant efforts on the part of those to whom the leadership of the schools of the nation has been entrusted, it has too often been a case of the blind leading the blind.

Efforts to cope with exploding enrollments, with building programs, with teacher scarcity, and with the routine and recurring tasks in school administration keep the school superintendent and his administrative staff on a treadmill. There are many districts such as are called to attention in Chapter 6 in which the superintendent is given sabbatical leave for professional study and opportunity to engage in workshops and institutes for furthering his own professional development. But because of the nature of his position, the superintendent, by and large, has not had the opportunity for travel and study which is urged upon the members of the teaching staff; and without some opportunity for renewing and replenishing the store of intellectual capital from which he draws, he can scarcely be expected to go on and on indefinitely inspiring a staff and stimulating a community of people to develop and support forward-looking educational policy. It is little wonder that school administration has failed at times to provide the educational statesmanship which is demanded of it.

Public education is not now or is it ever likely to be much better than its leadership. A state of growth, stagnation, or decay in a school district at any given time is dependent upon a series of challenges and responses. The challenges may come to the school system in any field—instruction, school buildings, personnel, public relations, curriculum, or any other aspect of the educational program. In a vigorous school system where the leadership is strong, the greater the challenge, the greater the response. But when the leadership, due to self-complacency or from lack of imagination or creative ability, is unable to arouse the school district and bring it to the point of successfully meeting the challenge, then decay begins. When this loss of vitality attacks administrative leadership, some leaders succumb; others manage to survive, but, exhausted, battle weary, frustrated, and disappointed, they are ineffective, and the deterioration which has attacked their leadership vitality is rapidly transmitted to the school system.[7]

The school administrator is faced with the necessity for solving highly complex problems that have social, economic, and psychological components. Certainly nothing could be more for the good of the schools in the district in which he serves than for him to be continually engaged in serious and deliberate study of the unresolved issues in American life—becoming familiar with the research in public school administration and related fields and analyzing the opinions and factual reports of scholars in a wide range of fields. The superintendency is reputed to be a lonely occupation. While no one can or should expect others to make the decisions for which a superintendent is responsible, school administration will come into its own only when every individual charged with administrative responsibility finds himself a working and learning member of something larger than himself.

## Administrators Who Engage in Inservice Education Are More Effective

Nothing said in this publication is meant to imply that administrators do not now engage in inservice education. Even those harried individuals who do not find the time or have the inclination to participate in conferences and professional meetings—as many of their colleagues commonly do—quite often peruse an educational periodical and frequently discuss some common problem with a professional friend or neighbor. However, the range in the amount of time and effort expended in this manner is so great that it defies explanation. The inservice education effort for a particular administrator and the type of inservice activities in which the administrator engages may vary markedly from year to year. Assuming that circumstances and personal choice may be responsible for much of this variation, any serious observer must conclude that there is little rhyme or reason to the over-all pattern of inservice education now engaged in by school administrators.

Most students of public school administration would probably agree that administrators of the better school systems participate in more comprehensive, ambitious, and numerous inservice activities than ad-

---

[7] Dimock, Marshall E. *Administrative Vitality*. New York: Harper & Brothers, 1959. pp. 50-51.

ministrators in less-favored districts. Whether some administrators have these opportunities because their school systems are better, or whether their school systems are better because they have the opportunities, is beside the point. The conclusion seems to be inescapable that, when there is participation on the part of administrators in professional growth activities, there is quality in the educational program. If this conclusion is correct, certainly no greater good could be done for public education in general or for local school districts in particular than to broaden and increase the participation of administrators in a sound program of inservice education; and the most important *single* thing that a school district could do to improve its schools would be to permit or, if necessary, require its administrators to engage in well-planned programs of inservice education.

A study made by Southwestern Cooperative Program in Educational Administration (CPEA) dealt with how some superintendents manage to improve their professional competence from day to day and to take advantage of many opportunities for inservice growth. This study accepted as a working hypothesis the idea that outstanding superintendents are those who have experienced marked growth on the job. A description of this study by Hollis A. Moore, Jr., concludes with this paragraph:

The interview data point to the conclusion that outstanding superintendents are distinguished by their genuine concern for continued professional growth. Their drive for inservice improvement is characterized by a sense of the intense importance of education and their ability to turn the conditions and experiences of their job into learning situations. They firmly reject the notion that the barriers to effective utilization of inservice opportunities are insurmountable. "It's not a question of whether you can afford the time for continued study," they said. "You can't afford not to." [8]

It may be that many boards of education who permit or encourage their administrators to engage in numerous professional activities outside the local district and beyond the day-to-day requirements of their administrative tasks do so because they feel some responsibility to contribute to the advancement of school administration and thereby to the general improvement of public education. It is likely that some are flattered by the favorable publicity such activities bring to the community. Others may believe that such publicity will cause local taxpayers to look more favorably upon the local school system. None of these are necessarily ulterior motives. However, the conclusion that

[8] Moore, Hollis A., Jr. "Forceful Incentives for Moving Ahead Professionally." *Nation's Schools* 51: 56-59; June 1953.

school systems in which administrators participate extensively in in-service programs and in professional activities *are* better school systems is strongly supported by objective observations, wherever they are made. Equally important, perhaps, is that individuals who experience inservice growth in the profession of school administration seem to prosper both in meeting the continuous challenges in their responsibility to the community and in the competition for better jobs and higher salaries.

## *Lay Organizations Need the Counsel of Informed Professional Leaders*

American society is noted for the number of its independent organizations. The American political system, based upon a permissive concept of government and on a pluralistic power structure, not only makes the development of voluntary organizations possible but it encourages them. The multiplication of associations is an outgrowth of cultural change and occupational differentiation. People in like circumstances seek associations with one another and tend to join in the pursuit of special interests common to the group. It is in the pursuit of these special interests that opinions are formed, concepts emerge, values take on shades of meaning, and action is initiated which shapes the character of institutions. In a word, these are the avenues through which the will of the people is expressed. These organizations, many and diverse as they are, constitute the very dynamics of a free self-governing society.

There are in this country, according to a report from the U.S. Department of Commerce, 1,800 national trade associations, 5,000 local chambers of commerce, and 77,000 labor unions.[9] There are 231 national organizations devoted, wholly or in part, to work on problems of public affairs and citizenship. The General Federation of Women's Clubs claims 15,500 member organizations and 850,000 individual members in the United States.[10] Warner identified 800 associations in a city of approximately 17,000 people. Of these associations, 357 proved to be permanent and important enough for study.[11] In almost every community of any substantial size, there are service clubs, veterans organizations, chambers of commerce, parent-teacher associations, and a host of other groups. In their programs, almost all of them give some attention to the schools,

---

[9] Judkins, Jay. *Directory of National Association of Business Men.* Washington, D.C.: U.S. Department of Commerce, 1961. p. 643.

[10] Gale Research Company. *National Organizations of the United States.* Detroit: the Company, 1961. Vol. 1, p. 643.

[11] Warner, W. Lloyd. *American Life—Dream and Reality.* Revised edition. Chicago: University of Chicago Press, 1962. p. 208.

and some groups—the parent-teacher associations, in particular—are primarily concerned with education.

Too frequently, when attention in such organizations is specifically directed to education, the program is limited to attempts by professional educators to describe or to demonstrate the schools' program. There is little or no opportunity for exchange of views between laymen and professional school people on the broad purposes and goals of the schools. Often, the time available is used in talking over specific incidents and minor problems not clearly identified with any general policy or purpose. It seems reasonable to assume that this lack of broad perspective and real purpose may be due, in part at least, to the failure of professional school administrators to look beyond the trees to see the forest. Charles R. Foster, in discussing the current challenges to educational leadership, says:

> Surely, most of the arguments have come up because people don't agree on our purposes. I am pretty sure that we can never completely settle on what they are. There will have to be compromises between or among differing theories. But I am also sure that any given school and any given school leader (teacher or administrator) must think this through and make certain what it is that *he* is for in education. Otherwise, there can be no leadership. We need to know what we stand for, and the public has a right to expect it of us.[12]

Demands for leadership that is effective in helping communities of people to determine a sense of purpose and direction in their educational program support the thesis that what school administration needs above almost everything else is opportunity for continuous study of the issues facing public education. Such opportunity should be a fundamental part of a program of inservice education for all school administrators. The superintendent, to a greater degree than anyone else in the school district, is in the center of the community educational scene, not as an interested bystander or casual observer, but as an active participant in the drama of community action on which the curtain never falls. Working with people in large groups, in small committees, and in informal conferences, he is advising, suggesting, and informing; calling attention to problems and needs just appearing on the horizon; pointing out half-hidden dangers that lie along different courses of action in time to avoid them;[13] offering constructive criticism in time to be helpful; giving

---

[12] Foster, Charles R. "Current Challenges to Educational Leadership." *Phi Delta Kappan* 43: 106; December 1961.

[13] National Education Association, Department of Rural Education. *The County Superintendent of Schools in the United States.* Washington, D.C.: the Department, 1950. p. 12.

bits of encouragement where progress falters because of doubts and uncertainties; and working with people in planning projects and activities through which they can get a fuller understanding of their community educational program—what it is, what it does, and the major goals toward which they want it to move.

These are critical points in the ongoing process through which a community of people gets ideas, forms opinions, develops concepts, and shapes an educational program. An educational program that is vitally alive and up to date cannot be developed or sustained for long apart from community life. More and more often, the superintendent is called into consultation with boards of health, planning associations, zoning authorities, and business organizations. These are focal points in community action—points at which the alert and well-informed superintendent's leadership is most needed and his influence is most effective in shaping attitudes toward public education.

Dean Keppel, in his address, "Public Policy and School Administration," commented:

> The profession of school administration will have to develop a more self-conscious attitude toward its role in helping to formulate public policy. The AASA, by its part in the Educational Policies Commission, has for many years been active in proposing policies for the schools. Yet I sense that it has not been the stimulating force that it might have been in demanding of its membership the analysis of the tougher issues of public policy . . . .
> If changes in training are the first steps, the changes in the climate of thought of professional associations are the second.[14]

Certainly, the Commission is not critical of the efforts of professional associations to grapple with the important issues of the day, nor does it regard them lightly. Rather, its concern is in strengthening such efforts and in making them more effective through an inservice education program that reaches every school administrator in the land. Such a program will not become a reality by wishing or by pronouncements of national commissions. A beginning toward this accomplishment will be made when thousands of school administrators in America become convinced of the need for an inservice program and national organizations such as AASA become committed to its implementation. As a first step, an inventory of the considerable offerings in inservice education should be made. Unnecessary duplication of effort should be eliminated and ineffective programs discontinued. These preliminary steps perhaps should be followed by ascertaining the pattern of participation by school administrators in general. On the basis of such studies, a coordinated

---

[14] Keppel, *op cit.*, p. 19.

effort among appropriate agencies might very well result in a reorganization of inservice education based upon sound objectives and an appropriate division of effort.

Speculation regarding an attempt to develop a systematic and comprehensive program of inservice education for school administration leads to other considerations of extreme significance. Problems that immediately come to attention are school district reorganization, proper administrative staffing, board-superintendent relationships, the role of professional educational organizations, and projection of long-range plans for capital outlay programs. These are problems about which there is often more talk than action. A vital program of inservice education could contribute substantially to their solution.

### Educational Research Must Be Expanded and Its Findings Widely Disseminated

Meager as educational research about the educative process, community organization, and promising administrative practices may be, there is little doubt that much of what is available never reaches people who would profit from it. In a publication entitled *Toward Improved School Administration*, the Kellogg Foundation states:

If practicing administrators are not promptly given the benefit of recent research findings and other contributions to knowledge, a considerable time lag exists between the discovery and use of this knowledge. And the problem of improving schools is too crucial to permit the existence of any great time lag. Therefore, there is an overwhelming need to transmit to the men on the job as much new knowledge as possible to enable them to carry on more effectively their work of improving the educational system of the United States and Canada.[15]

While the Commission agrees heartily with this statement, it does have some misgivings about "giving" administrators the benefit of research findings. Almost every administrator has more publications, releases, and research reports coming across his desk than he can give serious attention to. It seems paradoxical to suggest vast increases in educational research and, at the same time, to indicate that most administrators are not familiar with what current research there is. The solution to this perplexing problem lies, perhaps, in cooperative study in which school systems not only help determine the areas in which research is needed but also participate in the research program. This would be a significant departure from current practice in which much of the educa-

15 W. K. Kellogg Foundation. *Toward Improved School Administration*. Battle Creek, Mich.: the Foundation, 1962. p. 29.

tional research is carried on by candidates for doctoral degrees, with the schools as somewhat reluctant partners.

Where institutions of higher learning, foundations, state departments of education, and professional associations have launched studies of significant educational problems, they have usually found school systems interested and eager to participate. As a comprehensive inservice program for school administration develops, superintendents themselves should assume a large measure of responsibility for seeing that such projects become more numerous, that they deal with problems of major significance, that they be adequately financed, and that they involve a substantial cross section of schools and school districts of every type. Any progress that is made in this direction will be movement toward a genuinely worthwhile inservice education program for school administration and will be highly beneficial to the schools.

That the American nation is research-oriented in almost every phase of cultural endeavor except education is a phenomenon that is difficult to explain. Yet, education is a $15-billion-a-year enterprise with only a fraction of 1 percent of this money devoted to research and development. In *Oil Facts*,[16] a publication of the Committee on Public Affairs of the American Petroleum Institute, the assertion is made that during 1960, $289 million was spent by that industry in research and development on petroleum refining and extraction. The report goes on to say that the federal government financed $6.1 billion, or 58 percent of total industrial research and development, in all industries in 1960.

The participation of the federal government accounts perhaps in part for the manner in which expenditures for industrial research dwarf expenditures for educational research. However, there is another important factor to be considered. Most local districts are too small to mount a significant research project. Furthermore, few local districts are willing to share in bearing the expense of a study which may benefit all school districts. So most districts wait for someone else to do the research and to blaze the trail. Few school systems are, like the great corporations, large enough to proceed independently, and most of them are so involved in meeting immediate problems that press for solution that they have neither time nor energy left for basic research.

With responsibility for school administration and responsibility for keeping the educational program improving from year to year widely dispersed in more than 35,000 local school districts in 50 different states,

---

[16] American Petroleum Institute, Committee on Public Affairs. *Oil Facts.* New York: the Institute, November-December 1961. p. 2.

a grand strategy for research or a coherent design of advancement is needed. Any organization or institution or combination of organizations and institutions that wishes to move education ahead could hardly find a more fruitful area in which to begin than in educational research on a major scale.

## Inservice Education for School Administration Must Be Viewed as an Investment

The educational enterprise centers on people rather than on things. Its power lies in the intangible realm of relationships and ideas. Comprehension of the full dimensions and the true import of the task at hand —inventiveness, imagination, creativity, and the will to do on the part of people involved in the operation of the schools—gives a far greater thrust to the forward movement of the educational enterprise than any power derived from the material things with which it works. A shrewd entrepreneur in private enterprise, looking carefully at the force that is closest to increases in production, would seize the opportunity for making investments at this point as a way of increasing his returns.

In an editorial in *The School Administrator* of December 1961, Finis E. Engleman wrote:

> Industry after industry has found it profitable in recent years to give time off and pay expenses necessary for top administrators to attend short-term schools for executives. Some boards of education have likewise encouraged superintendents to pursue programs of study. Is it not time, however, for school boards generally to consider similar policies for their administrators?
>
> Nothing grows obsolete more rapidly than public education under the leadership of an administrator gone stale or unaware of the critical issues and changing demands on the schools. Even the good superintendent who reads, travels, listens, and confers with the best local minds can be stimulated and made more competent by temporary absence from his daily work routines and by induction into an environment of intellectual stimulation and deliberately planned contemplation.[17]

That the improvement and expansion of education has become a matter of national policy in most of the developed nations of the world hardly needs documenting. As a means of implementing progress in the developing nations, it stands at the top of the list. The American public seems to be committed to education as a prime weapon in the cold war. However, the *overtone*—and harassed school administrators could well believe the *very essence*—of this commitment is criticism of the achievements of the schools and of their efforts to solve difficult problems and an exhortation for them to do better. No substantial proposals for a

---

[17] Engleman, Finis E. "A School for Administrators." *The School Administrator* 19: 2; December 1961.

major breakthrough in public education have been embraced by the nation.

The quality of public education in America, to a great degree, depends upon the quality of its administration. Public school administration in America involves such a large number of persons that only a program built on a broad base of participation can be effective. In sports and, perhaps, with automation in business and industry, we are becoming a nation of watchers rather than a nation of doers. Without easily accessible opportunities for school administrators to engage in vigorous study and discussion of educational problems and issues—to engage in an inservice program through which they can continuously grow and develop —watching rather than doing could very well characterize the leadership of the schools.

Inservice education for school administration should be thought of as an investment rather than a cost. Every successful business corporation sets aside funds not only for capital investment but for personnel development. Every large business organization attempts to develop leadership among its own staff as well as to lure talent from its competitors. So far, the schools have almost wholly depended upon finding individuals who have planned and financed their own training or who have acquired the competencies needed through experience in some smaller or less desirable position. To the Commission, such practice does not make sense.

It would be good business practice and an expression of genuine confidence in the future of community education for every school district to set aside a portion of its budget for inservice education for school administration. This allocation of funds might be used for partially or fully paid leaves of absence for individuals currently employed by the district to enable them to engage in serious study of school administration. It might also be utilized to enable the district to participate in internship programs for active or potential administrators. A modest appropriation might go a long way in enabling a district to bring in consultants and resource people to help overworked administrators and their staffs assess their problems and develop comprehensive programs for improvement. The gains in insight and skills achieved by administrators rub off on the school systems in which they are employed. It is almost like casting a stone into the water.

Boards of education are constantly reminded that their most important task is the selection of a superintendent. However, they cannot select better superintendents than there are. Not until there is a professional group of practicing school administrators who are not only broadly educated but who are also engaged in a continuous study of the part public education can play in the solution of basic social and intellectual problems can our schools be as well administered as they ought to be. And until there is a sizable group of alert and growing school administrators, boards of education cannot expect the odds to be in favor of their securing the kind of leadership needed for their schools.

## The Will To Do

The vitality that all want to have in their educational programs and that many seek to have comes from the minds, hearts, and spirit of people. It is psychological in nature. It is the will to do something better; it is reaching for that which has not yet been accomplished. It is a strength which comes from unity of effort directed toward a goal not yet achieved. It is the courage to go beyond the tried and true and commonplace without abandoning it. These psychological forces do not reside alone with the school superintendent, the board of education, and the teaching staff. They are in the student body, the parent-teacher association, and in every other organization in the school district. The school superintendent, to a greater degree than anyone else, is the catalytic agent that arouses these intangible forces and leads them in a constructive manner toward developing and sustaining an educational program that everyone believes is good and that is getting better all the time. It is toward such ends and purposes that the inservice program for school administration should be directed.

# CHAPTER FOUR

# Administrative Problems
# Generated by Cultural Change

$S$CHOOL administration faces the challenges of an age in which the rate and magnitude of change are unprecedented. No single word more aptly describes this period of history than the word *change*. A modern counterpart of Rip Van Winkle, awakening from his 20-year nap, would think he was in a new world as, indeed, would be the case. All individuals, professions, and institutions are profoundly affected by the forces which make this the most dynamic and swiftly moving of all periods in history.

Of all our social institutions, perhaps schools should be the most profoundly affected by this transition since, in many respects, education is both an antecedent and a consequence of change. Schools cannot be understood, except in relation to the culture of which they are a part. The character of education is shaped by the society it serves; its aspirations, problems, and needs. The central purpose of education is to bring about change in individuals; for learning is change in the skills, knowledge, and understanding possessed by individuals, and as individuals change, the society they create inevitably changes. In his essay, *On Liberty*, written about 100 years ago, John Stuart Mill contended, "Human nature is not a machine to be built after a model and set to do exactly the work prescribed for it, but a tree, which requires to grow and develop itself on all sides, according to the tendency of the inward forces which make it a living thing."[1] The school that serves individuals and a free society best nurtures this growth by bringing every individual it touches as near as possible to the best he can be.

Education cannot be an uncritical agent of change, since its goals provide means for intelligently discriminating between good and bad

---

[1] Mill, John Stuart. "On Liberty." *Great Books of the Western World.* Chicago: Encyclopaedia Britannica, 1952. Vol. 43, p. 295.

change. This responsibility for critical evaluation and choice of directions leaves room for the preservation of essential stability in our society.

If education is to play the role thus implied, educational administration is extremely crucial in the continuous development and improvement necessary to make the schools adequate for the times. In a sense, this concept of function places administration at a crossroads. It must either choose to exemplify the superior leadership role demanded if education is to achieve its full measure of usefulness, or administration must abdicate this role to others. There is much evidence to show that educational administration is striving hard to function in the leadership capacities implicit in the nature of education's responsibilities. There is probably no leadership role in society more demanding or more complex. If educational administration is to be viewed as an intelligently critical agent of change, the requirements for continuous study are quite exacting. Those in administration must keep up with change, understand its causes and consequences, understand its proper impact on the schools, and be able to evaluate it and make intelligent applications of this knowledge and understanding to the schools and their own work.

The underlying concern of the AASA Commission on Inservice Education for School Administration and, indeed, of superintendents in every part of the land, is to make school administration an even more dynamic, positive, and effective force in dealing with the educational problems that lie ahead. Issues that confront the nation must be resolved, in the final analysis, by people who live in the neighborhoods, towns, and cities—in the local school districts—if democracy continues to be their way of life. The institution of public education for which the administrators and school boards in this country are so largely responsible is called upon to give them the skills, the knowledge, and the insights needed in grappling with the problems that lie before them.

School administration in the years ahead will gets its vitality not from the prestige of the office, not from the nature or the size of the administrative district, not from the salary the superintendent is paid or the manner in which the school board is elected, and not from the position the superintendent enjoys in the Rotary Club. Administration will become more effective and increase in stature and prestige as people throughout the length and breadth of the land come to know that superintendents and their associates are men and women who have breadth of knowledge, who have conviction, who sense that there is a mission to be performed in this country through the public schools, and who are fully committed to doing the job as well as possible.

The great strength of democracy is in its ability to muster the powers that reside in the hearts and minds of people and to bring them to bear effectively in dealing with the real issues before them—problems that transcend one's local environment, problems that are bigger than the individual, bigger than the family, that may be bigger than the community in which one lives, and problems that make people uneasy about some value they hold to be important. It may be the problem of insuring intelligent decisions at the polls, the impact of technology on employment, the opportunity for a college education, or the rights of teachers to participate in shaping policies that affect their working conditions.

Down underneath at sensitive points, these problems often jostle some of the values that people hold to be important. School administration must be alert to these issues, must comprehend them, and must see their implications for educational policies and programs. The distinctive quality of administrative leadership that the school superintendents in this country now have will be strengthened in the years ahead through better understanding of how these issues affect the lives of people.

School administration deals with people—some in school, some out of school. Every person that school administration touches has deep down in his heart a sense of values that is important to him. The rapidly growing population of this country is highly mobile. People are on the move from the farms to the cities, from the cities to the suburbs, and from one industrial community to another. School districts day after day are dealing with people who have been uprooted from a familiar environment and a comfortable life. Due to circumstances sometimes beyond their control, these people have been placed in an environment that is strange and frightening to them. The values that have stood them in good stead in their past lives and have given them a sense of security are shaken. Among them are farm children who feel cramped in a sixth-floor flat, restless youth reaching into an uncertain future, and men who have lost their jobs through technological developments. When people are thrown out of work, something happens to them. They have been hurt. And if their spirits are not completely stilled, they strike out at something which may be the school superintendent, a teacher, the curriculum, or a school-bond issue.

A simple population count reveals that something like 26 million young people will be coming into the labor market within the next decade. Unless opportunities for useful and satisfying employment are vastly extended, some of them will be grievously hurt by a cultural situation that they will inherit rather than build. Each and every one of these young people will have a core of values that will be important to him. The issues that come before them—whether they be related to unemployment, a political election, building a church, reorganizing a school district, voting on a bond issue to construct a new school building, or the content of the social studies program—will be dealt with on the basis of these values.

These are problems of democracy—problems that emerge in a dynamic culture—problems that call for careful thought, sober judgment, and resolute action. The purposes of the school cannot and should not be divorced from them. And the great challenge to school administration is to meet them with the same confidence, determination, and skill with which every problem of shaping the institution of public education has been met during the three centuries of its development.

What are some of the changes taking place in our society and in the world that dictate the need for a program of continuous learning for those engaged in educational administration? The purpose of this chapter is to set forth and briefly analyze some of the forces which call for continuous study and evaluation and which will undoubtedly make administration different tomorrow from what it is today.

### Some Cultural Changes in Process

Democracy possesses built-in dynamics of change. In contrast to a culture in which basic values derive from adoration of the past, democracy uses the past as a means of achieving a better future. Its essential values are always in the process of becoming, and its institutions are responsive to the will of the people. The premium American democracy places on the worth and dignity of the individual means that he should have the responsibility and the opportunity to develop his useful capacities to the maximum. "In proportion to the development of his individuality, each person becomes more valuable to himself, and is therefore capable of being more valuable to others. There is a greater fullness of life about his own existence, and when there is more life in the units there is more in the mass which is composed of them."[2] The examples of change cited here illustrate the dynamic qualities of a culture in which individuality and freedom of choice have been vigorously supported.

### The World of Work

Near a riverbank in an isolated rural area stands a $100 million plant which converts pulpwood into paper products. This plant is in operation

---

[2] *Ibid.*, p. 297.

24 hours a day, 7 days a week. Shutting down the machinery in the evening and starting it up again in the morning is just too expensive. Each shift of workers requires less than 200 persons. Each worker represents an investment in capital equipment of more than $1.5 million.

A trip through the plant is eye-opening. No human hand touches the raw material from the time it is brought to the plant until it is converted into finished products, machine-packed and labeled. The few workers are hardly noticeable in the huge plant; there are large expanses where no one is visible.

What do these workers do? They watch gauges and instrument panels and inspect the finished product as it comes off the assembly line. These people are unlike the factory workers of a generation ago, who were stationed along assembly lines doing work which was monotonous and deadening to the spirit and mind. Here, the monotonous drudgery is done by machines; the worker is a supervisor of technology in operation and an evaluator of the final product.

This new role for workmen requires a different kind of education. A man who is charged with responsibility for operating capital equipment costing $1.5 million per worker needs an education that is different from the education needed by a man whose total operating capital equipment is a pick or a shovel.

But the more dramatic stories of automation are not found in the industrial plant. The newer world of computers with electronic data-processing and record-keeping devices opens up new avenues of human achievement and employment. Problems can now be solved within a few minutes that formerly were impossible to solve or at best required months of painstaking effort in solution. Much routine clerical and book-keeping work is now done by electronic equipment.

The demand for and consequent growth in fields of personal service, while less dramatic, is nevertheless of profound importance. An increasing proportion of employed persons are engaged in service occupations ranging all the way from attendants at filling stations to highly educated social workers. New knowledge and the desires of the public for such services are enhancing their importance. In 1949, for the first time in history, the number of workers in service industries (transportation and public utilities, trade, finance, insurance and real estate, government services, and all other services) surpassed the number in goods-producing industries (agriculture, manufacturing, construction, and mining). Since then, the differential has steadily widened until by 1961, there were 34.4 million persons employed in the service industries and 25.2 million in the

48 INSERVICE EDUCATION FOR SCHOOL ADMINISTRATION

goods-producing ones. All indications are that the differential will continue to widen in the future.[3]

There is also a continuing and an accelerating growth in the need and demand for professional services. The number of professions is increasing, and specialization within professions continues. Preparation for a career in a profession is becoming more rigorous and demanding as new knowledge, pertinent to such preparation, develops with great rapidity. It is said, for example, that, if reports on the research done in biochemistry during the past year alone were placed on a single bookshelf, it would be 30 feet in length.

Thus, the world of work changes, and every change has its correlative in requirement from the labor force. There is less and less need for the unskilled worker and much greater need for the skilled and the professional. In 1961, 29 million people were employed in white-collar occupations as compared with 23.9 million in what are commonly called the blue-collar jobs.

The implications of these changes in the world of work for education are by no means clear at this time. Certainly, the nature and extent of vocational and professional preparation must be carefully reviewed. Questions concerning the need for continuing education and the type of continuing education, if people are to keep up with their own world of work, remain unanswered. Educational administration has an important role in determining answers to such questions.

*The Economy*

During the depression years of the thirties, the national income fell to a low of $40.2 billion in terms of current dollars. By last year, it had risen to more than $430.2 billion. The gross national product in terms of current dollars increased from $56.1 billion in 1933 to $521 billion in 1961. Measured in terms of the 1961 value of the dollar, the gross national product in 1933 was $146.3 billion. Changes in the world of work are largely responsible for the increase. Our capacity to produce goods seems virtually unlimited. We are no longer restricted by inadequate sources of power.

Hence, poverty is not necessary. It exists only because of lack of full national commitment to eliminate it. But the standard of living is moving steadily upward. Were it not necessary to spend such enormous sums on national defense, undoubtedly a great deal more could be done to reduce the incidence of poverty.

---

[3] Rosen, Howard. From unpublished materials of the U.S. Department of Labor.

The workers described above, behind whom is such heavy capital investment, are worth much more and are being paid more than were the workers of yesterday. Modern technology makes life easier and more pleasant and enables them to have a better standard of living. Their levels of expenditure, in turn, further improve the economy.

This new-found wealth with upward spiraling standards of living opens up new vistas for human achievement. More time for study is available, and more energy is left from the workaday world for new learning. Interests and talents hitherto undeveloped may now find expression in activities of people which are not directly associated with their daily work. There is time to think, time to reason, and time to create; there is a margin of human energy over and above the requirements for food, clothing, shelter, and defense that may be used to advance civilization a little further toward the highest aspirations and ideals of mankind; there is time to reflect on the pursuit of happiness and to seek ways to alleviate unnecessary pain and tension.

The extent to which more complete human development is possible rests in substantial measure on education. The new-found freedom made possible by our affluent economy calls for another dimension of education. The type of learning required is of a different order from the type required in preparation for the world of work. Its purpose is to help prepare the individual for maximum human achievement beyond demands of the world of work.

Just what this new dimension involves is by no means clear. The people of this country have pioneered in the development of an industrial society in which wealth and leisure have been broadly distributed. They have been firmly committed to material progress, but have intended that it be accompanied by an intellectual ferment that would strengthen the spiritual fabric of the culture. Now they face the question of whether cultural standards can be brought into balance with national well-being. This projects another unfinished task in which educational administration must play an important part. Gaining an understanding of the economy and the directions in which it is moving is one essential aspect of the preparation for this leadership role.

*Population*

During the decade of the thirties, analysts were predicting that population growth in the United States would level off at about 170 million persons by 1970. This estimate was, of course, based on trends which were then current. An unanticipated increase in birth rate trends has since occurred. A national population of about 325 million by the year 2000 is now predicted. While increase in the birth rate has been the major factor in population growth, a substantial addition has resulted from the growing percentage of persons 65 years of age and older. Hence, the pattern of population distribution by age is changing, with greater percentages at the extremes.

Advances in the science of geriatrics largely account for the increasing percentage of older people in our population. Improvements in child care and in medical treatment of the young help account for the increase in young people. Both groups, of course, have been helped by advances in nutrition and improved standards of living.

The development of metropolitan areas and the consequent decline in rural population have been watched with interest for a number of years. Within a few years, according to recent estimates, 87 percent of the population will be concentrated in about 40 great metropolitan complexes.

No one knows the full implications of these developments for schools and other social institutions, for the structure of local government, and for patterns of community living. Certainly, one aspect of this problem is the relationships of school administration to other departments of government in long-range metropolitan planning involving the location of school sites, water mains, sewage systems, highways, shopping centers—especially when the jurisdiction of several different governments is involved. The number of agencies and organizations in a metropolitan area that are directly concerned with school administration is rapidly growing. To illustrate, approximately 140 public approvals are required for the average community school building program in the state of California. This is an outgrowth of specialization and interdependence as the location, organization, and operation of the school become matters of serious concern to the highway department, the police force, the sanitation commission, the fire department, the health department, and other agencies of government that are responsible for the health, safety, and security of all citizens in the community.

The continued high birth rate spells out fairly clearly the quantitative educational load of the future. Much less is known about the quality and comprehensiveness of education needed. What is the significance of the great metropolitan complexes for education? Does the increasing proportion of high school graduates who go to college have any special meaning for the public school curriculum? the college and university curriculum?

The necessity for continuing education is probably no more dramatically illustrated than by the needs of persons who have reached the age of retirement from active participation in a profession or occupation. Thus far, our society has found little for the old to do except to die. Nursing homes are built for them, but constructive outlets for their energies and interests are lacking. This problem undoubtedly is one of the great challenges to education and to our developing society.

Changes in the number of persons in society, their age distribution, and the emerging patterns of population distribution have special meaning for the schools and their programs. The important role of educational administration in discovering these meanings and appropriately relating them to the schools can scarcely be overemphasized.

## Patterns of Living

Changes in the world of work, in the economy, and in the population are reflected in patterns of living. The stubborn process of replacing workers with machines repeats itself in every area of American life. Work and workers are transferred from the home and concentrated in offices, factories, and shops. A 13-year-old boy has only the vaguest idea of what kind of work his father does. He may indicate on his junior high school enrollment blank that his father is a process man at Standard Oil or that he works in the instrument room at Kaiser Aluminum, but he has no clear idea of what a process man does or what an instrument room is like. No longer does a father have opportunity to teach his son the occupational skills he needs or to guide him in developing attitudes toward the world of work. Society finds it expedient to keep millions of youth in school for longer periods of time—youth who previously would have been in productive labor. Not all of them are there from thirst for knowledge. Mass education, some contend, is only an alternative to mass unemployment. Few aspects of present society have been more widely discussed than the decline of old patterns of living and the evolution of new ones.

Concern for the role of the family has been paramount in these discussions. The decline in the strength of the family as a social unit has been widely discussed and greatly lamented. The place of children in the home has changed. There are few chores to do which draw the family together as a unit and which provide a type of training that many think essential in child development.

Millions of mothers are taken out of the home by employment in business or industry. Hundreds of thousands of fathers are engaged in work which requires them to be away from home much of the time. Former common interests and activities which tied the members of the family together in a strong social unit have been replaced by individual interests and services that may be purchased at a nearby shopping center. There are few opportunities for members to either work together or engage in recreational activities together. Outlets are sought outside the home. Members of the family align themselves with either formal or informal groups in accordance with their needs and interests. Such groups serve more substantial interests, too, inasmuch as they become spokesmen for their representatives and often function as pressure agents for a cause or causes. Among the prominent formal groups are labor unions and civic clubs. Informal groups are much more difficult to recognize, and their members are more homogeneous in interests since they are drawn together by personal contacts and relationships. This does not mean, however, that they are less important.

The extensive mobility of both families and individuals is a powerful influence on patterns of living. A substantial proportion of the people now live outside the state and even the region in which they were born. During the 12-month period, March 1959 to March 1960, 33.8 million people moved from one house to another; 11.2 million moved from one county to another; and 5.5 million moved from one state to another.[4] Many families have moved a number of times and have never settled down to become part of a community in the sense of community membership common to the generation of yesterday. People travel widely within and without the country. It is estimated that nearly a million Americans traveled outside the United States during the past year. This does not include military personnel.

The local community is far from the tightly knit social unit of yesterday when neighborliness meant that people worked together and helped each other. Communities of interest which defy specific geographical limitations have taken over many of the functions of the old local community. Social institutions, including the schools, are influenced by these changing roles.

Patterns of living are necessarily of profound importance to the schools and to educational administration. They have a bearing on educational objectives and the kinds of leadership needed. But these patterns of living must be identified and understood before their true meaning can be assessed in a local community.

What happens to school administration in this cultural ferment? Will it make needed adaptations in its processes and adjust to the changes which encompass it as community life becomes more complex and schools

---

[4] U.S. Department of Commerce. *Statistical Abstracts of the United States.* Washington, D.C.: the Department, 1961. p. 33.

grow larger? Superintendents in small, compact districts have felt a sense of security in having everything in their own hands. Transition from this simple, direct administrative process to administration through organization and group leadership is a step that is often difficult to make.

## Role of Government

Necessity has dictated the transition of government from a relatively laissez faire agency concerned primarily with maintaining an orderly society and defending it against outside threats to a powerful instrument for achieving national goals associated with a better way of life. Abraham Lincoln held that government should do for the people what needs to be done, but which they cannot do at all or do well through individual effort. Franklin Roosevelt saw government as a means for achieving the four freedoms which he so eloquently espoused. Even conservative forces which formerly strenuously fought implementation of this concept recognize that it now has a place in government.

The taxing power and policies of government have had great influence in redistributing wealth. Its power to regulate is employed in measures to control production, interest rates, and prices as means of achieving and maintaining a more balanced economy. Government has stimulated the development of transportation facilities—the railroads and more recently the airlines—and sought to preserve and to strengthen small business enterprises. Minimum-wage laws and efforts to achieve better working conditions and more satisfactory hours of work per week indicate similar goals of economic welfare.

Extensive legislation to care for the unemployed and the aged represents another area of government concern. The purpose of social security is to free the aged of much of their former worry about being able to maintain a satisfactory standard of living and to retain a measure of independence after their work years are over. Financial aid for the construction of hospitals and current interest in providing medical care for the old are other expressions of government concern for human welfare. The committee of distinguished economists and business and industrial leaders who wrote the Rockefeller report on the challenge to the American economic system held that:

The greatest advance in raising minimum living standards in the past generation, aside from the consequences of high employment and economic growth, has been made through social insurance. Under social insurance systems, employers and in some instances employees and self-employed persons set aside part of their current income to support programs which protect certain major economic events or hazards confronting individuals. These are, primarily, loss of income on retirement, during unemployment and during periods of temporary or permanent disability.[5]

The regulatory functions of government are also used to prevent harm to the common good by misuse of the power of big business. The quality of many products, particularly those directly associated with good health, is safeguarded by government inspection and regulation.

A more recent and rapidly expanding interest of the government is in support of research designed to improve the physical and mental health of mankind. Much important work is done in this area which in all probability would be left undone if it had to be undertaken and supported with private capital.

One of the most important questions concerning the future role of government has to do with its place in education. Historically, interest in education on the federal level has reflected deep concern about religion and morality—as expressed in the Ordinance of the Northwest Territory— and about a base of literacy for political democracy. Recognition that education is now a powerful factor in maintaining national security has created additional pressure to define more clearly federal responsibility for education. The manner in which the federal government should support education is a critical question that remains to be answered. What place will educational administration have in answering this and other questions concerning the future role of government in our society?

*Internationalism*

Future historians may well point to the determined efforts of downtrodden and underprivileged people throughout the world to improve their stations in life as a major characteristic of this age. The colonialism which failed for generations to bring to a substantial proportion of the world's population opportunities to achieve for themselves the freedoms poignantly expressed in the Declaration of Independence is being thrown off as new nations are born and new governments are instituted.

. . . in the course of a single generation, one sixth of mankind is transformed from all that is feudal and backward into all that is modern, advanced, and fearful. Political colonies are freed; new and less visible forms of imperialism, installed. Revolutions occur; men feel the intimate grip of new kinds of authority. Totalitarian societies rise, and are smashed to bits—or succeed fabulously.[6]

---

[5] Rockefeller Brothers Fund. *The Challenge to America: Its Economic and Social Aspects.* Garden City, N.Y.: Doubleday & Co., 1958. p. 53.

[6] Mills, C. Wright. *The Sociological Imagination.* New York: Oxford University Press, 1959. p. 4.

A restless and uneasy world peace hangs in delicate balance as two great ideologies struggle for the minds and hearts of men. The future of civilization and perhaps the fate of humanity hinge on the outcome of this competition. Cultural values and principles that have undergirded free societies take on new shades of meaning as the tempo of cultural change outpaces the abilities of men to orient themselves to its consequences. Cosmonauts racing around the earth in outer space is disquieting but convincing evidence that private enterprise is not the only way to make a society into a powerful industrial complex.

Since it no longer seems possible for one part of the world to prosper at the expense of another part, new patterns of international relationships must be developed. The emergence of the European common market holds promise. If this and other new patterns of relationships are successful, they must be based on a degree of mutual respect and trust which rarely has been achieved heretofore. Willingness of the strong and prosperous nations to help those who are less fortunate is also essential. It may be that new concepts of international trade will come into the picture, as now seems likely.

Few greater challenges face education and educational administration than those embodied in international problems and issues. These problems and issues range all the way from pressures to insulate ourselves against communism by refusing to learn about it in the schools or by viewing UNESCO as a communist organization to the problem of developing the kinds of relationships with all peoples that will bring about world peace in the true sense. Developing greater proficiencies in the use of foreign languages and shaping curriculum content so that the culture of many foreign countries is better understood places greater and greater demands on the schools. Education and educational administration must accept great responsibility for what is done to resolve these problems.

*Value Commitments*

The forces, the problems, and the issues which have been identified and briefly described above have their roots in transitions in our value commitments. Such transitions in values are reflected in the areas of change which have been discussed, and, at the same time, they are influenced by such change. This interacting relationship is extremely important and should be understood by the educator. Probably the most profound changes taking place in this country in this age are shifts in values that vitally affect the aspirations and the behavior of people and that disturb long-established ways of living.

It is perhaps paradoxical that, as the people of the country have achieved a considerable victory over former sources of insecurity—ignorance, poverty, and disease—new sources of insecurity have developed. A major source of this insecurity stems from international tensions and from the great struggle between democracy and communism. A sense of security is sought in increasing expenditures for the machinery of a global war that people fervently hope will never come. The attitude that one might as well live today as well as possible, for there may be no tomorrow, is a strange expression of this new insecurity. This fatalistic point of view appears to have influenced the development of a different attitude toward morals, a tendency to live beyond one's means, and a feeling that it is no longer wise to be frugal and to save for a rainy day.

One other factor influencing attitudes toward saving and living beyond one's means is undoubtedly the welfare provisions embodied in social security and unemployment legislation. The necessity for the individual to provide for his old age is no longer urgent. Whether or not this is a good thing is not our concern at this point. Reliance for security on resources beyond and outside the individual's own initiative and frugality is a factor which needs to be understood.

Critics have said that the American people lack strong national purpose, that they are soft people who are interested in easy living, and that they do not have strong moral fiber. Such critics advocate a hungry, belt-tightening, get-tough philosophy, especially when such measures would apply to persons other than those who most strongly advocate them. More vehement critics contend that the United States has developed into a welfare state which has undermined the individuality and spirit of independence so prominent in the earlier history of the country. However, few will deny that ample opportunities to pioneer in many fields still exist and that rugged individualism does not mean license to exploit others.

The reading habits of the American people are often cited as evidence that they are basically unintellectual and interested primarily in the gratification of their physical senses. Popular television programs, movies, and the popularity of observer participation in sports are used to support this point of view. Without attempting to assess the extent to which these charges are true, it can be pointed out that the values reflected in these tastes and cultural activities could be substantially elevated.

Perhaps a more important phase of our value transition, like some other areas of change, is not basically new, but an acceleration of long-existing trends. This phase has to do with the currently strong emphasis on achieving the ideals of democracy through extending its rights and responsibilities to all persons, regardless of minority relationships or racial origins. Everywhere there is a new search for the meaning of free-dom—the meaning of freedom as it is expressed in terms of opportunities for all individuals to develop their full potentialities for usefulness.

In spite of ambivalence in the value transitions noted above, there seems little reason for pessimism. The predominant weight of change appears to be oriented toward transmitting into practice long-held values concerning the worth and dignity of the individual. Where countertrends appear, they must be accepted as challenges to the vitality of the demo-cratic idea.

It is doubtful if any greater challenge faces education and educational administration than the problem of developing values for individuals and the culture. The one great truth that has been emphasized and demon-strated over and over again in the history of nations in all ages is that the values that undergird the culture cannot be taken for granted. Each new generation must see them with clarity and grasp them with vigorous intent. The forces which are influencing value commitments must be recognized and understood by the creative educational leader. Education cannot be neutral. It can have no purpose that is not derived from some set of values. One great need is to clarify these values and to make them explicit in developing school programs.

If educational administration is to demonstrate true leadership, it must accept major responsibility for establishing defensible value com-mitments, for the future of this country rests in the hearts and minds of men—in the ideals toward which they aspire, the purposes for which they reach, the firm commitments which they have made, and the ethical principles which they will not violate.

No informed person is unaware that the cultural revolution which has been briefly sketched here is influencing education and that, in turn, education is influencing this revolution. Education, more than any other social institution, must avoid complacency. The comfortable feeling that the schools are adequate for the current needs of society, that there is time for an easy breathing spell and for a bit of resting on the oars, is a luxury that cannot be afforded, particularly in this period of earth-shaking cultural change.

The forward-moving thrusts in science, in technology, in production of economic goods, and in social inventions for which the people of this country strive are all dependent upon the understanding, the skills, and the commitments of people. The vigor of institutions, the productive powers of industry, the quality of social justice, and the strength of the nation as a whole depend on the education of its citizenry. Each generation is called upon to meet the issues which confront it with the full measure of the skills and understanding it possesses. Education at every point is influenced by the forces which generate cultural change, and in no small measure, these forces determine what education is at a given time and the changes which are under way in its content, its methods, and its purposes.

Since the days of the early Dame school and the Latin grammar school in early colonial life, the goals of the public schools almost continuously have been in the process of redefinition. In periods of rapid cultural transition, momentary needs tend to receive priority. At the present time, the specific needs of a technological age—science, mathematics, languages, and research—are in the forefront of the discussion of the basic purposes, philosophy, and significance of the public schools in a free society. As pointed out earlier, the people of the country slowly have come to the realization that education is now a major instrument for survival in a world of competing ideologies. This realization is having a strong impact on public policy. A purpose of education for the individual has slowly evolved which is concerned with how well he is informed, how he thinks, his value system, and his over-all behavior as a human being. Further changes in educational philosophy and purpose may be expected in the society of the future.

These philosophical and purpose-centered transitions have profound significance for the curriculum. Current trends emphasize curricula which are more directly geared to achievement of the educational purpose which they serve. Involved is basic curriculum content—how it is chosen and organized and its relationship to educational outcomes. Even the mere modernization of curriculum content has proven to be a difficult task.

New discoveries in learning theory are being made constantly. When experiments show them to be superior to theories currently expressed in practice, teaching should be modified accordingly. Eventually, a fairly well-defined science of teaching may be achieved. All teachers are concerned with learning theory, and good teachers are anxious to reflect the best theory in their own work.

Much publicity has been given to new teaching devices such as teaching machines, television, and improved audiovisual equipment for classroom use. Some informed persons believe that a technology of teaching is developing. While current publicity tends to glamorize these changes unduly, there is no reason to assume that the effectiveness of teaching cannot be sharply increased through this technology.

Questions concerning the best organization for teaching constantly arise. Controversy exists over whether or not the use of mass media of communication for teaching necessarily violates long-accepted concepts of adapting learning to the individuality of the learner. Perhaps a more basic question is whether or not these media create uniformity in education and make more difficult the expression of one of the most widely accepted principles of learning: that the individual should accept responsibility for his own learning and should exercise initiative on his own.

Whether or not these media can be used to facilitate student exercise of the spirit of inquiry in learning remains to be seen. It is clear that there are numerous unanswered questions brought into focus by recent developments in education. There is also current serious concern for the evaluation of learning. Much popular interest centers on evaluation as judged by the mastery of a selected body of content, particularly in such popular fields as mathematics and the sciences. The relationship of this type of evaluation to those purposes of education which are rooted in behavioral outcomes is too often passed over lightly. Probably varying concepts of evaluation afford strong evidence of differences in opinion concerning the real functions of the school.

These and other areas of change which might be cited illustrate the need for administrators to know about changes which are under way, to understand them, to evaluate them, and to apply the results of their evaluation to educational practice.

### Changes in Administration

There has been somewhat belated recognition of the positive relationship of good educational administration to good schools. A tremendous amount of research and experimentation in educational administration has been carried on during the past few years. The W. K. Kellogg Foundation has invested more than $7 million in efforts to improve leadership in the schools. Results of these special efforts have made clearer than ever before the importance of educational administration in the development and maintenance of satisfactory educational programs.

Much current concern deals with efforts to formulate an acceptable theory of educational administration. This has turned out to be an extremely difficult job, and no generally accepted theory has thus far been articulated. However, there is no real reason to doubt that continued work along these lines will be successful. At any rate, there is now general acceptance of the concept that performance in educational administration should be rooted in some acceptable theory which deals with the basic role of administration in society, its functions in the school system, and the processes and procedures which it reflects.

The current changes of major importance in administration seem to consist of a shift from emphasis on control and management to more concern for leadership. Management is not viewed as being less important than before, but rather as being a part of the essential operation of good leadership. Educational administration, according to current concepts, should be imaginative and should be characterized by vision, creativity, democratic operation, and the sharing of responsibility. The current emphasis on leadership reflects a growing appreciation of individual worth and dignity as well as understanding of the value of the investment society has made in the professional preparation of teachers. The skills and power to stimulate and to hold the confidence and respect of a staff of people who are really top quality is a challenge that puts the conscientious administrator on his toes. Clearly, this is consistent with a basic purpose of education—the wise development of human resources. Administration can help people be creative by giving them opportunities and providing the necessary resources and services.

A second aspect of the current concern in educational administration is community leadership. Educational administration, while unique in many respects, is becoming increasingly important as a major segment of public administration. The unique responsibilities inherent in educational leadership pose special burdens on administration. These burdens have to do with community understandings, knowledge of community forces and their impact on the schools, community decision making, and the interpretation of education and educational needs to the public.

No scientific body of content is available on processes and practices in administration which truly reflect democratic concepts and which are effective in getting the educational jobs done satisfactorily. Experimental work in the future may well center on the development of content in these areas which can be accepted as definitive and valid.

Administration may be an emerging science of which educational administration is an important part. If this be true, survival of the individual in administration may rest heavily on how well he keeps up with developments in this science and their significance for his own performance.

### Value Orientation

The explosion of knowledge about which so much is being said and written today is a product of cultural revolution. The categorizations used here for purposes of analysis and description are by no means discrete; they are merely convenient ways of discussing the interacting parts of a cultural complex. There is an interdependence and a unity in society which is fundamental to teaching and learning. None of the forces identified here can be understood clearly in isolation from the others. Society must be viewed as a whole and dealt with in manageable parts. No better illustration of the relationships of the various segments of society to each other is available than its value transitions. Clearly, values are basic to any change and undoubtedly determine the nature of change. The brief overview given here is of a society in a state of motion, motion toward its goals. These movements are not fixed; their dynamics change from time to time; but basically, they stem from the underlying ideals to which people as a whole have dedicated themselves.

Some forces have been identified that bear on education and on educational administration. They are of national, regional, state, and local significance. Their impact varies from region to region, state to state, and community to community. Educational administration in the local community must see these forces as they operate locally and their relationship to state, regional, and national trends.

There are few who doubt that new kinds of education are needed and that more education is essential. It may be that people will need educational services throughout their lives; the nature of these services will be strongly influenced by the forces which have been discussed.

Thus, these forces will help to shape the schools of tomorrow. The concept of educational administration implicit in this chapter requires that it assume major responsibility and leadership in extending the horizons of formal learning.

The emergence of a new educational administration is evident in local school systems, intermediate districts, state departments of education, and on university campuses. It concerns itself with all of the forces here described and others suggested. It views itself as leadership and conceives its major function to be that of releasing available potential to provide the programs of education which the problems of individuals and society need. This places the administrator in the thick of decision making, not only within the school system but within the whole community, thus increasing the importance of his role in the total community.

How is this role to be achieved? How may educational administration constantly improve its competence in discharging this role? Recently, an entirely new course was developed and introduced in the curriculum of an engineering school during an academic year. The justification for this course was that so many new discoveries had been made recently in the field of engineering that the course was needed immediately to replace that which had become obsolete in the curriculum.

It would be difficult indeed to imagine a profession in greater need of a carefully planned and well-thought-out program of high-level services to prevent obsolescence than educational administration. If the profession truly aspires to the leadership role about which it talks, this program for continuous learning is essential. Educational administration is itself an agent for intelligent change, an agent which can be justified only because it enhances achievement of the better life to which education is dedicated. It can succeed only as it changes, also.

# CHAPTER FIVE

# Guidelines for Shaping
# the Program

$\mathbf{E}$ZRA CORNELL commented at the opening of Cornell University, "There is not a single thing finished." This ringing challenge to a great university in its infancy, so aptly expressed in this terse and simple phrase, is echoed in school systems throughout the length and breadth of the land. The final answer to most school problems—whether they be in the field of curriculum content, instructional methods, personnel policy, business practices, pupil guidance, school plant construction, internal organization, or school-community relationships—is never acquired. The professional growth of the superintendent and members of his staff is never completed. The responsibility of the school district for increasing the understanding, broadening the vision, stimulating the growth, and developing and perfecting new skills and new techniques on the part of all people—administrators and teachers, custodians and maintenance employees, bus drivers and cafeteria workers—is never entirely met. In school district responsibility, there is always room for improvement, there are always items of unfinished business.

## The Basic Purpose

The basic purpose of a program of services to administration in a school district—if the program is soundly conceived and well designed—is to bring to the district, at strategic points, the additional measures of leadership needed to keep the total school program moving forward and upward toward a higher level of accomplishment and more effective performance. It provides the factual information, the insight, the know-how, the encouragement, and the will to do—essential to making improvements whenever and wherever they can be made. It helps people help themselves. In a sense, it helps the school with its unfinished business in the area of staff development and improvement.

A soundly conceived and well-executed program of services for school administration gets information in usable form to people who are responsible for the schools and for what they do. Its purpose is to help them come to a clearer understanding of any and all aspects of an ongoing program of education. An effective program of services adapts the results of research to local conditions and initiates further research where additional information is needed; works with people rather than for people; involves the acceptance of ideas and suggestions on the part of those who are directly served as well as the offer of practical assistance by those who provide the service. The highest ideals, the noblest concepts, the latest research findings, and the best-known practices remain sterile and barren until they are truly reflected in the thinking, planning, and action of people; until they become a functional part of the intellectual working equipment of people; and until they are accepted, assimilated, and used with confidence, ease, and assurance. This process of gathering ideas and putting them to work has been the road to progress in every field of cultural endeavor. This is a promising road to progress in the further improvement of school administration. "In-service programs should be organized and developed with full recognition of principles of learning that long experience and well founded research have proved to be appropriate and effective in the classroom."[1]

The design of an effective program of services for local school district administration must be something more than a neatly drawn organization chart listing the names of paid personnel and indicating the flow of responsibility. It must be more than an operational plan that is peddled among school districts on a fee basis. It must be more than a series of off-campus courses offered each Wednesday night in county-seat towns. It must be more than semiannual visits of an inspectoral nature to school districts by state department personnel. It must be more than surveys made when authorization for an issue of school bonds is in the offing or the schools are under attack by overly severe critics. The program must be tailored to fit the needs and situations peculiar to the district in which it operates. It must be deeply rooted in the conviction that the people in the district—administrators, teachers, school board members, lay citizens, everyone who is concerned with the schools—are more important than bonds, buses, buildings, and budgets; and that real improvement in any aspect of the school district operation will be made only as changes take

---

[1] Gilchrist, Robert S.; Fielstra, Clarence; and Davis, Anna L. "Organization of Programs of In-Service Education." *In-Service Education for Teachers, Supervisors, and Administrators.* Fifty-Sixth Yearbook, National Society for the Study of Education. Chicago: University of Chicago Press, 1957. pp. 285-86.

place in the knowledge, understanding, viewpoints, and skills of people. Bringing about desirable change in people must be the focal point of its organization and operation and the motivating force that sustains the program of services and carries it forward.

A soundly conceived and well-designed program of services to administration in a school district deals with the what, the why, and the how of current operations. It begins with problems that worry, disturb, and annoy people, with problems that limit their effectiveness, with questions to which they are seeking answers, and with issues which they themselves believe to be important. It helps them to do better the jobs immediately before them. It brings the right information to bear on the problem at the right time. It stands up well under the ultimate test of usefulness. In serving the program of the school district, it operates for the improvements it can make, for the growth in vision and understanding on the part of people that it can engender, and for the good it can do. There is no problem of major consequence in the school district—whether it is related to custodial services, school-plant construction, curriculum revision, personnel policy, or evaluating the daily work of pupils in the classrooms— that is not the concern of the school superintendent. In joining with the people immediately involved in thinking through them and finding the best possible solution, the superintendent grows professionally and, in turn, adds to the quality of administration in the schools for which he is responsible. This is the essence of an inservice program.

Being primarily problem centered, the inservice program is, nevertheless, not disdainful of organized subject matter materials, nor does it treat them lightly. Quite to the contrary, it uses subject matter and research findings extensively, but uses them for clearly discernible purposes. Drawing on the content of many disciplines, it helps people in the school district and, in particular, the superintendent and his immediate staff with the all-important function of clarifying purposes, establishing goals, and developing commitments.

Every great administrator is moved and guided by unshakable convictions, profound faith, and clearly defined purposes; and every outstanding educational program reflects these moving forces. To instill this inner driving power in the administrator and in all with whom he works is the great end of an inservice program. The artist may know all the properties of oils and paints, fully understand the subtle effects of colors and shadows, and have superbly mastered the technical skills involved in their application; but unless he has an all-important purpose that he wants to achieve and a deep-seated commitment that he has to fill, and unless he keeps faith with himself, his work will be shallow and of little consequence. This principle of purpose and commitment, so fundamental in the artistry of inanimate materials, is far more compelling in the artistry that shapes the lives and molds the delicate spirits of children and youth. To help administrators, teachers, school board members, and the lay citizenry of the school district clarify purposes, establish goals, make commitments, and fully resolve to keep faith with themselves and to meet the responsibilities placed upon them is the highest purpose of a soundly conceived and well-designed program of services to a school district.

## Strategic Points

There are two fundamental points that must be kept clearly in the forefront in the planning, development, and operation of any program of services, whether it be conceived on a state or a regional basis. These points, each vitally related to and dependent upon the other, are the recipients of the service, on the one hand, and the agencies, organizations, and institutions which provide the services, on the other. The guiding principles and criteria which shape the program and give it content, character, and flavor exist in the intricate network of relationships that obtain between these two crucial points. To fail to give full and careful consideration to either in the development of any program of services is to launch it upon a wave of uncertainty and uneasiness, where its effectiveness is seriously limited and its chances for continued success are seriously impaired.

It will be the school districts, for the most part, that will be seeking and receiving services of various types. At the present time, in most parts of the country, it will be state departments of education, colleges and universities, professional organizations of school people, and privately operated survey and research agencies that will be providing the services. Wide variations in such factors as density and distribution of population, character of school districts, location of institutions of higher education, proximity to the state department of education and research agencies, ease of travel and communication, availability of financial resources, established practices and precedence, and the nature of the problems and issues confronting school districts at any given time make it impractical and perhaps impossible to establish any set of specific criteria or principles that is applicable at all times and all places. Discretion and judgment must be flavored with common sense at all times. This is the essence of the statesmanlike leadership that must be exercised in developing and sustaining effective programs of services to school administration.

As the leadership essential for developing and sustaining continuous programs of services to school administration that is demanded by the forward march of cultural events and the growing desire of professional school people in every facet of the organization and operation of schools further develops and becomes more active, attention will be focused sharply on such crucial points as—

1. *Initiation.* Circumstances must prevail wherein it is relatively easy to get inservice programs under way. The approach must be simple. Requirements must not become unduly restrictive, establish precedence, exclude innovations, or limit creative and forward-looking action. The lid should be taken off and people given a chance to do what they know needs to be done.

Numerous illustrations could be given of where such procedures are followed at the present time, but the following single example illustrates what is already being done to good advantage in one state. In Georgia, many county superintendents who are responsible for the administration of local school districts are elected by popular vote. Four years ago, people without previous experience as school superintendents were elected in 20 school districts. While the incumbent superintendents whom they had defeated in the election were without doubt highly professional people, they felt no compelling reason to spend a lot of time orienting the people who would replace them. The newly elected superintendents knew little about budgeting, personnel policy, working with a school board, handling public relations, purchasing materials and supplies, accounting for expenditures, and handling the recurring problems involved in the maintenance of a school plant. With these simple housekeeping problems of school administration in mind, this group of 20 men turned to a professor of education at the University of Georgia and asked him for assistance.

Pleased with the request, the professor offered to assist them if they would organize study groups in four sections of the state where he could meet with each group for a six-hour session once every two weeks. Somewhat to his surprise, the study groups were formed within a relatively short time, and the professor promptly set out on the circuit. The schedule of meetings was sustained throughout the year and has been continued over a four-year period. Through this inservice program together with some summer sessions on the campus, each man in this group has met the full requirements of the University of Georgia for a master's degree in school administration, and, at the same time, has developed into an effective school administrator.

The essential point in this illustration is that there was available on the University campus a man who had the know-how and the time available to assist men and women who needed help with the immediate, vital problems that confronted them. By dealing with the problems in a constructive manner, the stature and professional competencies of the men and women increased, and school administration in these several districts was better than it would have been otherwise.

The initiation of an inservice program need not always come from individual superintendents. It may come from people in the school district, from a professional organization in a region or a section of the state, or from the state department of education or a college or university. The important point is that the initial steps not be so difficult or so complex that people who really need help or who are in a position to give important service are discouraged from taking them.

2. *Planning.* Responsibility for planning any inservice program should be shared by those who receive the service and those who provide it. This is fundamental. If local school districts assume full responsibility for planning, they may tend to look for packaged services that can be bought from the lowest bidders and may fail to comprehend the full possibilities for educational growth in the problem or situation immediately at hand, whether it be planning a school building, developing a new system of reporting pupil progress, or revamping the content of the social studies program. They may fail to see the full potential of the educational services that are available. They may fail to visualize the full dimensions of the problem or issue which leads them to ask for assistance. On the other hand, if the agency or institution that provides the service assumes full responsibility for planning, the service may well become a kind of dole system with services and neatly organized information dribbled out at the pleasure and will of the dispenser. Such stock-planned programs of services, designed and developed without primary consideration for the people who will use them, may lack the essential ingredient of vitality that can come only from an intimate and intrinsic relationship to the interests, concerns, and needs of the people in the local district.

The Agricultural Extension Service, operating over a period of 40 years in an inservice program to an important segment of the culture, has effectively demonstrated the advantages of cooperative planning. Through common working arrangements, the federal government, the land-grant colleges, and the governing boards in practically every county in the United States have joined in instituting and operating a program that has

revolutionized agricultural practices and led to levels of production that
have become a problem because of abundance rather than paucity.

Wise administrators will avail themselves of all possible consultant
services in the development of programs of services to the personnel in
their districts. One superintendent, in commenting on this planning
function, said:

Some superintendents try to play the part of specialists in all directions when in
truth they know very little about some of the highly specialized features of the
educational program. Such superintendents will serve their districts better, in my
opinion, if they seek to identify the specialists in these fields and call on them for
assistance.[2]

There is no simple and sure-fire approach to planning the content,
scope, and nature of a service program, but some school systems have
established administrative councils which have direct lines of communication to the individual teachers and principals and supervisory personnel
in the districts. These councils have proved to be very effective in
identifying needs in the school district and developing operational plans
for programs of services that will meet these needs.

3. *Finance.* The inservice program should be so financed that nobody
in the state will be deprived of services essential to the effective operation
of the schools in the district because of lack of funds. This is fundamental.
It is frequently the school district with the less-adequate staff, the less-
seasoned leadership, and the least amount of money that needs such
services most. To bypass them or to count them out just because they
have no funds is to seriously weaken the whole concept of an inservice
program at its most vulnerable point.

Evidence at hand at the moment indicates that inservice programs to
school administration should be jointly financed by the state, the local
district, and the service-dispensing agencies if they happen to be tax-
supported institutions. When the local district, through its policy and its
action, fully accepts the concept that investment in the professional
development of school personnel is a reasonable and a justifiable approach
toward adding quality to the instructional program, it is reasonable to
assume that some budgetary appropriations will be specifically earmarked
for this purpose. Local circumstances will affect the amount of this
appropriation, but, undoubtedly, a strong case could be built for making
it 1 or 2 percent of the current expense budget.

Tax-supported institutions of higher education unquestionably have
some responsibility for the well-being of the total culture of the state.

[2] Curtis, William H. Letter to the Commission, October 30, 1961.

This principle is one of the fundamental bases for their creation and support through public tax funds. This responsibility has been accepted and met in an admirable manner by many institutions in such fields as agriculture, economics, political science, and public health. Where this responsibility has been met, these institutions have had budgetary appropriations which permitted the employment of personnel and the development of off-campus and on-campus programs essential for meeting the responsibility. With the growing importance of education, there is ample reason for contending that school administration should be supported by public institutions of higher education in a comparable manner. And there is equal reason for contending that state departments of education should assume greater measures of responsibility for the professional growth and development of school superintendents in their respective states as a positive and direct approach toward improving the quality of the instructional programs for which the state is ultimately responsible.

Funds must be available from some source for initiating action, for probing into new territory, and for demonstration purposes. Until people have a clear concept of what can be done over and above what they are already doing, they can only make progress through the slow and expensive process of trial and error. Developing such experimental programs, carrying on pertinent research, trying and testing innovations, and demonstrating procedures and possibilities are some of the fundamental elements in the leadership process. Unless provisions are made in a scheme of financial support for such activities, the program of services to school administration will fall short of its true purposes.

4. *Orientation.* The inservice program should be indigenous to the locality in which the service is rendered. It should fit the situation. It should be applicable. Its orientation should be in harmony with the philosophy of the school district. It should be related to problems that actually exist, that are real, that are alive, and that are of vital concern to the persons receiving the service. An inservice program is not likely to be effective if it is built upon make-believe or imaginary problems.

There are many examples of research in education today that lack vitality, that are superficial, that fail to reveal information that teachers, principals, board members, and superintendents need to deal effectively with vital problems confronting them. There are innovations in school buildings, in instructional methods, and in internal organization for administrative purposes that are developed in abstraction and huckstered to school districts without any fundamental consideration given to the circumstances in which they will be used or the purposes they are expected to serve. Where such practices in approaches to improving the schools are followed, the principle of local control is isolated.

Few people would deny that there is a uniqueness about community life reflecting ethnic backgrounds, family relations, leadership patterns, value systems, technological development, and financial ability. These factors should be as clearly reflected and as fully considered in the inservice education program as they are in the curriculum content and the instructional methods of the school district.

5. *The Point of Beginning.* To start where the people are—a well-established principle of teaching and learning—is as essential to an inservice program as it is to any other aspect of the educational enterprise. The inservice program should allow time for growth in understanding, step-by-step progress in the modification of practices, and a gradual approach to the reshaping of purposes and objectives.

If it is to have real educational value, it must function on a long-term basis. Ready-made packaged answers and quick solutions to questions and problems that are peddled by any service-dispensing agency have little part in an inservice education program. If it is truly inservice education, it leads to learning. And learning on the part of professional staff members, on the part of a board of education, or on the part of a community of people covers a time span not wholly unlike the time span required for a child in the first grade to learn to read.

6. *Know-How and Knowledge.* An inservice education program that limits its purpose merely to the development of know-how falls far short of its full purpose. Know-how suggests routine operations, mechanical manipulations, recipe-following, technical performance. It suggests the laboratory technician, the radio repairman, and the machine operator. All are important in their respective fields, and all have important counterparts as individuals and as processes in the organization and operation of a school system and in the teaching and learning process. But they fall short in suggesting the depth of understanding, the broadness of vision, the organizational ability that judiciously weighs alternatives, the uncompromising commitment to an ideal or a purpose, and the creative imagination so essential to shaping and directing the course of public education and to giving it its deeper tones of character and quality.

The inservice education program that is not fully committed to imparting knowledge and understanding as well as to developing know-how is not worthy of being well supported or long sustained.

7. *The Individual.* The individual's role in an inservice program, particularly if he is the superintendent, must be an active one. He must

want to profit from his experience. He must want to grow. He must be willing to give unsparingly of himself for this purpose. He must stand ready to make sacrifices of time, money, and effort. If he is not so constituted, he must cultivate himself to the point that he gets satisfaction from probing deeply into problems and issues, into experimental research, and into a great variety of factual information. This is a price that must be paid for real professional improvement. It has been said long ago that there is no royal road to learning. No inservice program can be conceived or operated that will negate the fundamental principle expressed in this simple phrase.

8. *Personnel.* The people who take major responsibility for making the contacts and providing the cluster of services that constitute a total inservice program to school administration must be capable, thoroughly informed, and highly successful in working with mature people in informal situations. The principals, the superintendent, and the supervisors with whom they will be working in an inservice program are leaders in their own right. Day after day, they are right on the firing line of an ongoing operational program. They are keenly sensitive to live problems and issues. They are, so to speak, under the guns every day. They have to make decisions, they have to act, they have to take responsibilities, and whatever they do and however they perform their tasks has a telling influence on the lives of the people to whom they are responsible and on the character of the institution which they serve.

Working with people of this kind is entirely different from the more leisurely pace that can be set with a classroom of undergraduates on a university campus. The people who accept leadership responsibility must be able to inspire confidence, prove their worth, make sense in all they do and say and suggest, and clearly demonstrate that they have a reservoir of leadership power and professional strength from which the people who come in contact with them can draw freely and find themselves refreshed and strengthened.

9. *Credit.* The problem of granting credit for work done in an inservice education program cannot be treated lightly or sloughed off easily. As administrators and other educational leaders in school districts in every state are motivated toward further professional growth, and as standards are set by certification requirements, criteria for employment, and membership in professional organizations in terms of a degree or a specified number of college hours, it is sheer nonsense to pretend or to assume that the ablest people in the profession will not want to meet these requirements. And it is equally nonsensical to believe that any great percentage

of them can leave their positions and their responsibilities for a full year or two to meet these requirements. This is a reality that must be faced.

Over a period of many years, institutions of higher learning in this country that have major responsibility for the preparation of educational leaders have emphasized and moved toward programs that would bring graduate students onto the campus for relatively long, uninterrupted periods of work as a means of adding depth and quality to the preparation programs. They have clearly seen the advantages that come to graduate students through associations with faculty members and other graduate students, through frequent conferences and discussions that are a part of university life, through use of library resources and laboratory equipment, and through getting caught up into the movement and tempo of life in a graduate school and becoming a part of it for a long period of time.

Off-campus activities in the nature of extension classes and study groups of relatively short duration, when used as a basis for meeting the requirements for a degree or for certification, have been considerably in conflict with the movement toward longer periods of on-campus study. The recent AASA constitutional amendment requiring two years of graduate credit in an institution approved by an accrediting agency has accentuated this problem. The standards set by the accrediting agency have leaned heavily toward a minimum of one year of on-campus work as a basic requirement in an approved program. There are many able superintendents in the field whose present qualifications are not equal to the standards set by the profession to which they belong. That they want to meet these standards is unquestionable. But to leave their positions for a full year is impossible in many instances. The men and women in these strategic positions are the people upon whom the responsibility for educational leadership in the years immediately ahead rests to a greater degree than on any other groups of people of comparable number. To fail to give them the full opportunity for professional growth that they want and ought to have is to reflect a weakness in the administrative ability and in the character and quality of the institutions of higher education in this country that does not exist. And, on the other hand, to move indiscriminately toward developing a program of off-campus activities that will meet the needs of these administrators may seriously weaken the preservice preparation program that colleges and universities have so assiduously sought to strengthen during the past decades.

There is no simple answer to this perplexing question. Universities, state departments of education, state associations of school administrators, local school boards, and individual school superintendents must join in working toward the solution of this important problem. Sabbaticals, leaves of absence, specially designed programs, and considerable self-sacrifice on the part of many individual superintendents will undoubtedly all be fundamental factors in any progress that is made toward solution. Undoubtedly, there will be many features of a well-planned inservice program that will meet the most rigid requirements for college and university credit. But meeting requirements for college and university credit is not the business or the intent of the inservice program. It has been demonstrated over and over again in this country that to the extent to which credit hours become a primary concern in an inservice program, the inservice program loses its vitality and its real reason for being.

10. *Flexibility.* The element of flexibility is predominant in any inservice program that is problem oriented and adapted to the needs of local districts. Cooperative planning opens the way for flexibility that may be achieved through a wide variety of approaches. In some instances, concentrated seminars that bring administrators together on a university campus for several weeks for depth study of major problems and issues may be the most effective approach. In other instances, one or more staff members from a university or state department may meet at regularly established intervals with staff members in the local district to work on a particular problem. In still other instances, the program may take the turn of action research, regularly scheduled off-campus course offerings, surveys, or work projects leading to the development of plans for a new school building, revision of a course of study, or improvement in the methods and procedures of evaluating and reporting pupil progress.

At the present time, universities are often cooperating with local districts through internship-type programs for developing administrative and supervisory leadership. The important point here is to adapt the program to the job that needs to be done rather than to fit the job into a predetermined program of services. A college relations committee at one state university has been successful in securing a small grant of funds to bring together in a nearby school district at regular intervals throughout the year outstanding people from all over the country to meet with the professors of school administration and the superintendents in the general locality. Most of the leaders invited to take part in these seminars are outside the field of education. They are sociologists, psychologists, political scientists, scientists, anthropologists, and scholars of the humanities. The professors of school administration and the superintendents join as equals in this inservice program in transferring the ideas and concepts from these disciplines to an educational setting.

In developing an inservice program, care should be exercised in attaching a hierarchy of values to any of its aspects. Anything that is worth doing is worth doing well. When a service, whatever its nature or extent may be, truly meets the needs of the personnel in a school district and truly leads to substantial professional growth and improvement, it is a valuable service. If it does not meet these criteria, then it should not be offered. Educational leaders who have responsibility for planning, directing, and sustaining inservice programs should keep in mind that experience in dealing with a live problem in a classroom, in a school administrator's office, or in a community setting may be as effective and rewarding as any experience in a laboratory or within the classroom of a university campus.

11. *Team Spirit.* People who seek assistance and receive help through an inservice program should not get the impression that they are being talked down to or that they are being regarded as unequals of the people providing the service. A true team spirit—a spirit that is more than make-believe—must prevail. It must be genuine. Personnel going out from a state department of education, from a university, or from any other service agency to assist administrators and teachers in a local district who do not have such an attitude toward the people with whom they work had much better be given other assignments, for they will do more harm than good.

12. *Simplicity.* An inservice program is likely to be most effective in its early stages if it is simply organized, if it avoids undertaking too many things at once, and if it does not become involved too early in a problem or issue that is so complex and so intricate that a long span of time will be necessary to arrive at any appreciable goals. There is nothing that stimulates learners, whether they be mature people or children and youth, more than some tangible evidence that progress is being made, that some worthwhile achievements are taking place.

13. *Resources.* The inservice education program should draw on a wide variety of resources—information, materials, and personnel—outside as well as inside the field of education. It should, when the program calls for it, seek out and use freely personnel with expert knowledge in business, industry, agriculture, medicine, and law and personnel in labor organizations, government, and research institutes to add to the storehouse of information administrators and other school personnel draw on

from day to day. It should draw heavily on the broad disciplines of science, economics, history, philosophy, and literature in helping people gain new perspectives, establish goals, and form commitments.

Paradoxically, with the growth of knowledge and increased specialization, the thoughts and experiences of men are drawn into narrower and narrower channels. Their actions, far too often, are circumscribed and limited by the pressures of the task immediately at hand and the requirements of their field of specialization. The work they do becomes more and more specialized, and the books they read tend to be in their own fields of specialization. The personal acquaintances they seek and cultivate are with people who work at jobs comparable to their own.

Opening windows on new cultural vistas and giving the professional personnel of the school district new and deeper insights into the forces that motivate youth and adults and shape the ideals and values by which their actions are guided are a continuous and compelling leadership challenge to the school superintendent that is never fully met. Giving administrators practical assistance in meeting this leadership responsibility is a function of the inservice program that must be in the forefront of the thinking of those who shape it and direct it.

14. *Policy.* After careful study and deliberation, the local school board, following the recommendations of the superintendent, should adopt a policy that establishes the general framework within which an inservice program can be developed and operated. This policy should indicate broad purposes, authorize the use of funds and facilities, and provide for appropriate participation of personnel in the school district in the inservice program. This policy should be well publicized so that people in the school district will clearly understand the ends to which school funds allocated for this purpose are being used and be fully aware of the special efforts school personnel are making to improve their professional competencies. Such understanding is essential if the inservice program is to become a well-grounded part of the total educational program of the school district.

15. *Payoff.* The inservice program must stand up well under the rigid test of usefulness. Citizens of the school district, school board members, and, most of all, the administrators and other professional personnel must be fully convinced that the time, energy, and financial resources devoted to the inservice program are yielding real benefits and adding strength to the educational program at points where it is most needed.

## More Specifically

In its totality, a broadly conceived and well-planned program of service to school administration includes human and material resources, organization and procedures, and clearly formulated purposes. In translating these purposes into a program of services, the points which will serve as useful guides to action are—

1. Insist that local school boards adopt policies to govern the in-service program.

2. Clearly establish the purposes of the program in the initial stages of planning.

3. Involve in the planning process the people who receive the services as well as the people who provide the services.

4. Tailor the program to fit the needs of the particular district in which it will operate.

5. Begin with problems that worry, disturb, and annoy people.

6. Start where the people are, and allow time for growth.

7. Work with people rather than for people.

8. Help people help themselves.

9. Keep the organization simple.

10. Develop the program on a long-range basis.

11. Work toward the development of a policy which makes financial support of the program a joint responsibility of the state, the local district, and the service-dispensing agency.

12. Make it easy to get a program of services under way.

13. Establish a basis of financial support so that no district will be deprived of services for lack of funds.

14. Avoid financing the program through charges per credit hour to individuals.

15. Bring the right information to bear on the problem at the right time.

16. Maintain flexibility in the program.

17. Seek out and use people with expert knowledge outside the field of education.

18. Help people to do better the jobs immediately before them.

19. Be content with small beginnings, and move step by step into more complex problems.

20. Employ service personnel who can inspire confidence and make a real contribution.

78

21. Treat people who are receiving the services as the equals of those who provide them.

22. Draw on the subject matter content of many disciplines.

23. Provide funds for probing into new territory and for demonstration purposes.

24. Recognize that a learning experience in an informal community setting may be as effective as a learning experience in a formal university setting.

25. Place responsibility for giving credit or declining to give credit on the institution that provides the service.

# CHAPTER SIX

# An Overview of Inservice
# Programs Now Under Way

INSERVICE education programs for school administration of varying types and of varying quality are in operation in each of the 50 states. Through a rather extensive survey, the AASA Commission on Inservice Education for School Administrators has identified a considerable number of these programs, and in this chapter describes some of them in detail.

No attempt was made in this survey for anything like complete coverage. Furthermore, the details involved in reporting made it impossible to include descriptive statements of many of the programs that were called to the attention of the Commission. The intent here has been to select types of programs as illustrations of what is being done by colleges and universities, state departments of education, professional associations of school administrators, and local school districts. These illustrative programs will serve well as guides to the further development of inservice programs for school administration beyond points which have already been reached.

This survey was made by directing inquiries to approximately 250 educational leaders—heads of state administrative groups, state school boards associations, and schools of education in public and private institutions of higher learning throughout the United States. In the initial inquiry, the attention of these educational leaders was directed to the responsibility of the Commission. They were invited to report programs now under way. Although the response from these educational leaders was not 100 percent, a broad sampling of practices was secured from representative areas of the country. The reaction to the Commission's assignment, expressed in statements by many leading educators in which they pointed out the great need for continuing inservice programs, was most encouraging.

## Institutions of Higher Learning

Because of space limitations, the initial section of this chapter is confined to a detailed study of the organization and operation of an inservice program in one university. This descriptive report is followed by pinpointed descriptions of more specific aspects of inservice programs in several other institutions of higher learning.

### A Diversified Program

The inservice program for school administration at Indiana University can well be characterized as working together toward a common purpose, cooperating in planning, and sharing responsibilities. The University's Division of School Administration, its Bureau of Field Services, and its Placement Bureau work closely with the State Department of Public Instruction, the State School Boards Association, and associations of school administrators on a wide variety of educational undertakings, problems, and issues. The Division of School Administration is responsible for preservice preparation of school administrators, placement of administrators and teachers, and provision for other services as needed by school corporations. The director of the Division and his staff have established rapport and communicate effectively with practitioners in several organizations of school administrators. For example, the director of the Division works closely with the Indiana Association of School Administrators. Another staff member spends half of his time serving as the executive secretary of the Indiana School Boards Association and the other half of his time as professor of school law. (Headquarters for the Indiana School Boards Association are located in the University's School of Education.) Another staff member serves as chairman and sponsor of the Indiana North Central Association of Colleges and Secondary Schools, and still another acts as sponsor of the Indiana Elementary Principals Association.

Effective communications help to identify problems and to call attention to the inservice needs of the men and women in the field and on the job. Inservice programs have been provided through extension classes, school surveys, workshops, consultant service, and publications.

*Extension classes.* Classes in specific areas of school administration are offered for the convenience of practitioners on week nights and Saturdays, both on the campus at Bloomington and at the 10 extension centers operated by Indiana University throughout the state. Many of these classes are organized as seminars and are problem centered, so that members of the class are able to bring actual problems in school administration to the group for discussion or to present possible solutions to problems to the class for critical evaluation. Recently, an out-of-state group of 25 administrators petitioned the staff of the Division of School Administration to offer three semesters of graduate courses at an extension center near the Indiana state line so that members of the group could work toward a specialist's degree. The school welcomed this opportunity to contribute to the improvement of school administration and, at the same time, to assist individual administrators in qualifying for higher degrees.

*School surveys.* Many Indiana school administrators turn to the Division of School Administration for intensive and extensive school surveys. The administrators become members of the survey teams which make objective studies of geographic, sociological, economic, population, and educational factors that are vitally related to school administration. These studies extend over periods of time varying from three months to two years and lead to recommendations for district programs, facilities, and plans for financial support.

*Workshops.* Each year, many school administrators attend and take active part in a number of short conferences or workshops. Among the workshops which have been in operation during the past few years, there have been school building conferences, school business managers workshops, beginning superintendents conferences, school administrators conferences (regional and state), postlegislative workshops, and the Indiana School Boards Conference. In 1961, a conference was held in conjunction with the National Organization of Legal Problems in Education (NOLPE) which was meeting in Indianapolis. Thus, cooperative planning gave school administrators and board members in the state an opportunity to discuss many problems and provisions of school law with the NOLPE members.

*Consultant service.* Specialists in school law, school finance, school-plant planning, school-community relations, school business management, and state and federal administration receive many requests to serve school districts in an advisory capacity. This service ranges from a two-day study of the administrative structure in a newly reorganized district to a two-year study involving administrators, staff members, and lay citizens in the preparation of educational specifications for a new building project.

The University's school-plant planning specialist has served as a consultant to school systems in Europe and in Asia, and in this work has provided inservice education for administrators abroad. Other staff members are regularly assigned to serve in Thailand as part of the fulfillment of the University's contract with the government of that country.

Specialists in school administration have worked with state-wide groups of lay citizens on various problems of school finance and school district reorganization. In one instance, these specialists spent two years working with citizens of the state on proposals for legislation which led to the enactment of a semipermissive school district reorganization law. As a result, a state-wide program is now under way to reduce the number of school districts in the state to approximately 250.

The Indiana Department of Public Instruction frequently calls upon members of the faculty of Indiana University's Division of Administration to assist with state curriculum studies, to advise in developing formulas for distributing state school funds, and to assist in supervising special programs. In addition, arrangements have been made for doctoral students in school administration to serve as interns in the State Department of Public Instruction.

Through a cooperative arrangement, the School of Education and the College of Arts and Sciences employ curriculum coordinators to work closely with the school system in the state in improving academic programs. Coordinators have been employed for the language arts, foreign languages, science, and mathematics.

*Publications.* Research bulletins and special publications are frequently prepared by individual staff members. Practicing administrators have also been involved with the faculty in the preparation of such publications as the handbook for the Indiana school administrators. An example of a publication designed to improve school administration is *Setting Our Sights.* This booklet is for school administrators and the 92 Indiana county reorganization committees at work on redistricting.

*Immediate and long-range concerns.* In commenting on the University's inservice education program in general, the dean of the School of Education says, "Although we are greatly interested in contributions to research and to the pre-service preparation of administrators, our program is strongly oriented toward the direct and immediate improvement of administration in the public schools."[1]

---

[1] Shane, Harold G., dean of the School of Education, Indiana University, Bloomington, Indiana. In response to the Commission's inquiry.

Many of the institutions responding to the Commission's inquiry reported continuing programs comparable, in many respects, to the inservice program at Indiana University. Most of these programs operate within an area in relatively close proximity to the University.

## Regional Study Groups

Superintendents in the state of Virginia meet regularly in five regional groups to study problems affecting public education. Members of the staff of the School of Education, University of Virginia, act as advisers to four of the groups. The chairman of the Department of Education, College of William and Mary, advises the fifth group. Each group acts independently in planning its programs and projects, but, in instances when the advantages are readily discernible, two or more groups plan joint programs. A major function of the study groups is to help busy superintendents keep abreast of current developments in American education. Staff members from the University of Virginia and other institutions of higher learning are called upon to lead discussions and to act as consultants. Sometimes, groups sponsor visits to school systems to observe and study new and improved educational programs, instructional techniques, and new plants. A member of the University staff reports that one such study group of school administrators has met monthly over a period of more than 30 years.[2]

## Advanced Administrative Institute

The executive director of the Center for Field Services, Graduate School of Education, Harvard University, in reporting on the inservice educational program at this institution, called attention in particular to the Advanced Administrative Institute. Due to the nature of the program and the limitation of facilities, attendance at this Institute is by invitation only. In the foreword of the 1961 Institute bulletin, the purposes of this program are described as follows:

The Advanced Administrative Institute grew out of the recognition by the Graduate School of Education of the need for programs particularly aimed at the practicing school superintendent. Ten summers have passed since this conception became a reality and the wisdom of hindsight appears now to have more than justified the origination of the Institute. Those comparatively halcyon days when Arthur Bestor was the only critic on the educational landscape have long since passed into antiquarian interest as crisis upon change upon pressure have radically re-oriented all of us to different conceptions of the administrative task.

---

[2] Holmes, George W., III, School of Education, University of Virginia, Charlottesville, Virginia. In response to the Commission's inquiry.

Through the years, the programs of the AAI have mirrored these changing conceptions. In the early days, AAI programs tended to focus on discrete managerial tasks confronting administrators. Programs concerned with educational reporting, public relations and communications reflected those conceptions of the administrative task classifiable under such rubrics as "maintenance" or "stabilizing." With the soaring of Sputnik, the emphasis changed toward "quality" and "change." In 1959, the focus at the AAI was on innovations in curriculum practices, while last year the concern was with the quality of leadership in a changing environment. That the AAI should be a product of its social milieu is neither a damning nor condoning comment, but simply an inescapable reality. Increasingly, however, those responsible for planning the programs have been exercising a prerogative of looking more and more into the future.

The future, as we see it and as the theme of the 1961 AAI suggests, will demand among other things that educators have an easy familiarity with the findings of the various social sciences and an understanding of the thought processes and methodologies of these disciplines. While this necessity has been heavily underscored in recent years, it is, frankly, doubtful whether the social sciences have made any deep inroads into the daily goings-on of our school systems. In a way, this is strange since the quantity of relevant materials from the social sciences is both impressive and overwhelming. The variety of conceptualizations that have sprung from studies of bureaucracy, leadership, personality, bargaining and exchange, data processing, power systems, cross-cultural investigations, decision making, and small groups offer fertile research and theoretical models for administrative testing and application. It has been suggested that perhaps the understandings required to study a situation differ from those demanded in acting in a situation, and this difference explains the failure of the findings in the social sciences to transfer to the realities of administrative practice.[3]

*Practicums*

The School of Education, University of Miami, works with the Dade County (Florida) Public Schools, which are in close proximity to the university campus, in a series of self-study practicums. The leadership for each self-study practicum is vested in the school principal, with the county school supervisor and a university professor serving as consultants. Participants may earn academic credit, and the program may involve the total faculty of the school. The practicum sets the stage for continuing inservice education under the principal's leadership. Although geared to include teachers, a significant outcome of the practicum is the inservice growth of the administrator—including the development of his security in his leadership role.

*Seminars*

As in many universities located in the direct environs of a large city district, the School of Education, University of Miami, cooperates with the

[3] Harvard University, Graduate School of Education. *Perspectives for Educational Change.* Cambridge, Mass.: Harvard University Press, 1961. p. 3.

Dade County Public Schools in conducting seminars for school adminis-trators. These seminars meet on alternate weeks over the entire school year and offer graduate academic credit. Inservice education of the Miami school system's administrative personnel is a major objective of these seminars. The work in these seminars involves—

1. Wide reading of professional literature.
2. Discussion of major issues in education and analysis of criticism of the schools.
3. Study of research and promising practices.
4. Application of research to local school problems.
5. Development of criteria for use in the evaluation of school practices.
6. Consideration of world problems in relation to the schools.
7. Revision of existing curriculum guides.
8. Production of administrative guides and shaping of policy state-ments.
9. Using standards of accrediting groups and other standard criteria in evaluating current practice.

*Social Science Institutes*

The University of California at Berkeley sponsors a series of social science institutes. These institutes are designed to increase the adminis-trator's knowledge and understanding of the social sciences which under-gird the practice of school administration—economics, sociology, social psychology, and public administration. Participation in these institutes is limited to 35 selected superintendents.

As an illustration, a University faculty member, in describing an insti-tute program devoted to economics, pointed out that the purpose of this particular institute was to provide a new kind of instructional program in economics for school superintendents which avoided nonessential jargon and details and brought understanding to such vital but puzzling issues and questions as—

1. What are the social goals of our economy?
2. Why do we continue to have periodic recessions?
3. What tools do we have for fighting recession?
4. How much annual growth does our economy need?
5. What comes first—the rise in price or wages?
6. Can we pay high wages and compete abroad?

7. What's all this talk about the gold flow?
8. Is social security an insurance program?
9. Can we afford luxuries *and* slum clearance?
10. Federal Reserve and Treasury—which does what?[4]

## A Clearinghouse

The School of Education, University of Denver, through its Bureau of Educational Research, works closely with the Rocky Mountain School Study Council in an extensive and continuous program of services to school administration. Through this cooperative working arrangement, a clearinghouse for information and ideas pertaining to the work of all phases of school administration is maintained. School administrators in the entire Denver metropolitan area are involved.

## Liberal Studies Program

The Center for Continuing Education at the University of Georgia sponsors a number of programs for groups concerned with school administration. Of particular interest is the Adult Liberal Studies Program. This broadly conceived program, organized under the subtitle, "The Basic Issues of Man," probes deeply into the philosophical principles and systems of values of the total culture. The program is divided into six major areas: the Nature of Man, the Social Life of Man, the Political Life of Man, the Scientific Life of Man, the Artistic Life of Man, and the Philosophic Life of Man.

For each of these content areas, there is a specially prepared book and two specially prepared half-hour films based on partial contents of all the books. The program, however, is not concerned with the use made of this material for its own sake; rather, it is concerned with its use by the participant in understanding fundamental cultural problems and in establishing bases upon which they can be met in an intelligent manner.

The program will require six week-end residence periods at the Center, during which time the participants will meet in small groups with trained leaders to discuss problems under study. The participants will view, either on television in their homes (over the University's educational television station) or by film in special locations, the 13 half-hour

---

[4] Reller, Theodore L., professor of education, University of California, Berkeley, California. In response to the Commission's inquiry.

films (two films for each of the six content areas, plus an introductory film). They will read the six special texts, plus additional readings that may be chosen from the selection of collateral reading which will be made available to local libraries. The primary aim of the program is to stimulate adults to begin and to continue a liberating education.

The multitude of perplexing problems—problems that call for deep insight into the behavior of people as they live and work together, problems for which there are no exact answers, problems which can be dealt with only through the use of subjective judgment—come with recurring frequency to the superintendent's office, to the school board meeting, to the faculty conference, and to informal community forums. This program is intended to help people put these problems into proper perspective and to instill a sense of order and purpose in what men do.[5]

*Resident Seminars*

The University of Chicago has initiated a series of resident seminars for superintendents. The underlying purpose of these seminars is to clarify objectives and to reassess procedures in the schools as they face the tremendous task of organizing into comprehensible form the increasing bodies of information in mathematics, science, and the social studies. Institutes and workshops for the inservice education of school personnel, university officials contend, have become commonplace. For the superintendents of schools who must guide the whole process of converting the work of the scholar into a form in which it can be effectively used in the instructional program, however, there has been little help other than conferences and clinics of short duration.

As an initial step, the Division of Administration of the University invited a limited number of school superintendents—about 20 drawn from the length and breadth of the United States and Canada—to spend October, November, and part of December of 1962 on the campus in full-time resident study. These men were given leaves of absence for this period by their respective boards of education. Their full salary and, in most instances, university tuition fees were paid by the participating boards. Attendance was limited to superintendents who received personal invitation. It should be pointed out here, not as a criticism but as an indication of need, that the cost of this program automatically eliminated administrators from most small school systems.

---

[5] Masters, Hugh B., director of Continuing Education Center, University of Georgia, Athens, Georgia. In response to the Commission's inquiry.

*Interinstitutional Workshop*

The Interinstitutional Workshop at Michigan State University is a course that will be expanded to include inservice training for selected administrators in the state of Michigan. This unique program has been organized and is conducted to give school administrators opportunity to meet distinguished scholars and great leaders from all over the United States and from other countries of the world face to face and to engage in direct give-and-take discussion with them. There is a significant difference between hearing an outstanding scholar lecture to a large audience and having this same person discuss problems with administrators around a conference table. The planning committee that initiated this program believed that motivating administrators into higher dimensions of thought would be one effective way of upgrading the profession of school administration. The danger that the school superintendent will be captured by routine activities and never have the opportunity to raise his sights to larger and more important purposes is always present.

The Flint school system will in a measure become a pilot center where distinguished scholars, well-recognized authorities, and practicing administrators will look critically at the operation of the school system against a background of critical cultural issues of the time. In follow-up procedures, an effort will be made to apply what is learned and observed in the Flint conference in day-to-day operation of the local school systems from which the participating superintendents come.

*Research*

A state research committee in Michigan, working in conjunction with institutions of higher education, has been organized to study educational issues on a state-wide basis. A coordinator from the State Department of Public Instruction, who is qualified to direct the research activities of all cooperating agencies, makes special effort to bring to the attention of skilled research workers problems of real concern to administrators. This organization will look critically at the preparation program for teachers and administrators as well as at teaching and administrative practices in the field. Also, the coordinator and research scholars will analyze and recommend ways to remove roadblocks that impede educational progress in communities. A university faculty member states that "in the past we have had very little factual information to rely on when discussing educational matters. Now it may be possible to tell where we are in the teaching-and-learning process and to see steps that need to be taken to move from where we now are to where we ought to be."[6]

Through this research effort, geared to the organization and operation of the schools, salient facts can be made available to board members, legislators, and key citizens in the state. Not only will this permit school administrators to present the problems, needs, and achievements of the schools to the public in a more effective manner, but the process of working together will be a stimulating experience as well.

*Interdisciplinary Seminar*

Michigan State University operates an interdisciplinary extern class for practicing school administrators and persons training for school administration. This class meets in week-end sessions, beginning at noon on Saturday with afternoon and evening sessions and continuing through a noon luncheon session on Sunday. The meeting place is alternated between the Michigan State University Biological Station at Gull Lake and the Conservation Training School at Higgins Lake. These two camps are situated approximately 200 miles apart in ideal locations on beautiful lakes, away from the hustle and bustle of campus life. Each site has full room, board, and recreation facilities. Outstanding people in education, communications, industry, philosophy, and other disciplines make presentations and join in the discussion at these meetings. The membership of these extern classes includes veteran school administrators, beginning school administrators, secondary principals, elementary principals, and graduate students training for administrative positions. The group thinks through and reacts to problems in government, human relations, social control, power structure in community life, curriculum content, leadership, and cultural change. Provisions are made in the work schedule for individuals with common interests to meet in sections to discuss the information and ideas gathered in the larger central sessions. Sessions of these extern classes may be scheduled on the University campus when the principal speakers and consultants cannot come out into the field or when the group would like to share them with an even larger group.

*Conference on Administrative Problems*

Of the many continuing inservice programs sponsored by Teachers College, Columbia University, the annual conference on administrative

---

[6] Campbell, Clyde, professor of education, Michigan State University, East Lansing, Michigan. In response to the Commission's inquiry

problems of superintendents of schools and other administrative and supervisory officers is perhaps best known. This is an invitational conference, with membership limited to approximately one person per state. Local boards of education are encouraged to pay the expenses incurred by their administrator in attending. Through intensive day and evening sessions, six days a week for a three-week period, the participants work with outstanding resource persons from communications, government, political science, science, banking, and education. They have an opportunity to hear the presentations and to discuss the ideas projected. In these conferences, a whole new world of concepts is opened to the superintendent, particularly the superintendent from the small school system who tends to become submerged in the life of his own school system.

*Associated Public School Systems*

The Associated Public School System is another inservice organization developed as a nationwide, nonprofit organization of 240 public school systems, study councils, colleges of education, and state departments that operate as a unit of Teachers College. This association carries on research, disseminates its findings, and reports information to its members. Teachers and research workers throughout the nation, as well as administrators, are involved.

*Other Programs*

Auburn University, Boston University, the University of Connecticut, Fresno State College, the University of Michigan, Western Michigan University, the University of Mississippi, the University of New Mexico, the University of North Carolina, the Ohio State University, the University of Tennessee, and West Virginia University reported quite extensive inservice programs. Space limitations prevented their inclusion here. Again, it should be pointed out that the inquiry by the Commission was not directed to all institutions of higher education. Had the coverage been complete, there is good reason for believing that many other programs of a comparable nature would have been identified.

**School Boards Associations**

Reports of inservice programs from state school boards associations emphasize cooperation with state associations of school administrators, institutions of higher learning, and state departments of public instruction. This working relationship was well expressed by an executive secretary of a state school boards association who said, "We have joined in a number of projects with our association of school administrators in the belief that whenever school board members meet, the superintendent of schools should be present."[7]

*Work Conferences*

The Michigan Association of School Boards combined its 1961 annual meeting with the fall meeting of the Michigan Association of School Administrators. In this working conference, 1,500 board members, 500 school administrators, and 800 wives and other interested lay representatives listened to the outstanding speakers this larger conference could afford, joined in smaller group discussions of current educational issues, and studied educational exhibits.

The long-range plans of the school boards association indicate the intent of establishing this working conference as part of a continuing inservice program for board members. The MASB, with the Southwest Michigan School Administrators Association as cosponsor, also schedules a state-wide, three-day working conference at Michigan State University each January. Here, teams of board members live and work together with their superintendents at the Kellogg Center, probing into questions pertaining to the school curriculum rather than discussing finance, salary schedules, and legislative problems as is so often the case in such meetings. The insights gained through living and working together in this atmosphere, with authorities in the field serving as consultants, enables board members and administrators to take back to their home district a better understanding of their working relationships.

Late in March each year, the state school boards association cosponsors with the University of Michigan and five other state universities a state-wide, one-day working conference. A series of board training institutes that reaches one-fourth of the counties in the state are scheduled at the county level each year. School law, the role of the school board member, and development of school policies are usual topics for discussion in these institutes. In meetings scheduled in July and August following elections, attention is specifically directed to the new board member and good "boardsmanship." The state school boards association also sponsors 32 state-wide study committees, with membership on the committee equally divided between board members and other lay citizens.

---

[7] Wettergren, W. A., executive secretary, Minnesota School Boards Association, St. Peter, Minnesota. In response to the Commission's inquiry.

*Publications*

To keep Association members informed, the *Michigan School Board Journal* is published monthly. Bulletins and periodicals on current legislative problems, curriculum developments, and other topics of interest to administration are published throughout the year. It is in no sense an exaggeration to say that the Michigan Association of School Boards works hand in hand with the State Department of Public Instruction and with the foundations and institutions of higher education in a continuing program of inservice education for school board members and administrators. The state office operates a lending library for local boards, where current literature in the field—copies of school policies, contracts, salary schedules, and other pertinent materials—can readily be obtained on request.

The staff of the Association is surprisingly small, numbering only five persons, but they receive considerable professional help from the state universities, the State Department of Public Instruction, local board members, and administrators which enables the association to make a notable contribution to the program of inservice education in this state.

### Professional Organizations

There are 81 formally organized state associations of school administrators in the 50 states. In each of 22 states, there is but one association. In each of 26 states where county superintendents and local superintendents have separate organizations, there are two associations. One state has three associations, and one state has four associations.

Annually for the past 14 years, the presidents of these associations have been invited to meet together with the elected officials and Headquarters staff of the American Association of School Administrators to discuss problems and issues of common concern to the total profession and to project plans for action for the coming year. These annual conferences, in effect, have been concentrated workshops for leadership training. The growing vigor and effectiveness of state associations can be attributed in no small part to the exchange of ideas, to the new insights gained, and to the stimulation received as leaders of state associations work together in these annual conferences.

State associations of school administrators are—to a greater extent than in former years—feeling and accepting responsibility for the profession of school administration. Professional standards, ethical practices, preservice and inservice programs, working conditions, contractual agreements, community status of the school superintendent, and admission into the profession are becoming matters of concern to state associations of school administrators. No longer is the superintendent waiting patiently for the character and status of the profession to which he belongs and to which he devotes his life to be determined solely by legislative action, state department of education directives, and the fickle whims of community sentiment. He sees the school superintendency as a position with competence and dignity—a position in keeping with the importance of the responsibility assigned to the key leader of a community educational program. He deems it essential that this leader possess thorough professional preparation and have firm commitment to purpose. The professional leader joins his associates in state associations of school administrators to accomplish these purposes. Professional status for an individual or for a group of people engaged in the same occupation is not something that is inherited or legislated into being, nor can it be created by pressure tactics. Professional status is a high sense of community respect, trust, and confidence that is won and held through exercise of a high degree of competence and firm commitment to a purpose. It is toward such an end that the 81 state associations of school administrators are slowly, but consistently, moving.

## School Management Institute

The School Management Institute (SMI) is a permanent organization that was developed over a five-year period through the cooperative efforts of the Ohio Association of School Administrators and the Ohio School Boards Association. It is governed by a board of directors comprised of 12 members—6 from each of the two organizations which founded the Institute.

The main purpose of the Institute is to provide for and coordinate the continued professional development of school administrators and related personnel concerned with the operation of educational institutions and organizations and to keep the administrator informed about refinements and innovations in management methods as applied in the field of education. The intent of all its programs and activities is to put at the disposal of practicing school administrators the best knowledge, techniques, and skills which can be gleaned from education, business, and industrial management.

SMI seminars and clinics cover the field of school personnel administration—job descriptions, staff organization, evaluation, appraisal, and new job orientation. Going beyond personnel problems in the seminars, intensive study is made of communications, public relations, and administrator-school board relations. While the program consists in large part of short, concentrated seminars, a complementing program of research guides and supports the Institute. At intervals, complex problems of administration are thoroughly studied and reports published under SMI auspices. The Institute is comparable in some respects to the American Management Association, which provides services for business and industrial management. The Institute is strictly an inservice program for the on-the-job administrator. For this reason, seminars and clinics requiring a minimum of time away from school activities are scheduled and developed.

## Area Study Groups

The Texas Association of School Administrators and the Texas Education Agency work together in a state-wide project for the improvement of school administration. This project was begun in 1955 by dividing the state into 28 work-project areas. In each area, there is an organization of superintendents to direct such activities as summer conferences, workshops, study groups, and a state-wide curriculum study. Services of consultants from colleges and universities, strong public school systems, and the Texas Education Agency are utilized. Publications produced include 10 study guides for school superintendents, guides to instruction in 10 subject areas, and a handbook for school board members.

## State Educational Agencies

Many state departments of education join with institutions of higher education in sponsoring institutes, workshops, and conferences for school superintendents, school board members, principals, and supervisors. These programs usually take the form of annual state-wide conferences devoted largely to planning, annual orientation conferences for new personnel, drive-in conferences held periodically in various sections of the state, and staff conferences with administrators and supervisors in local school districts. Specialists from state departments of education work with superintendents in regional and zone meetings in planning legislation, in establishing workable criteria for school building construction, in developing curriculum guides, in planning research projects, and in developing criteria for use in the reorganization of local school districts.

## Educational Conference Board

The New York State Department of Education has worked effectively for many years with the Educational Conference Board in this state.

This is an agency composed of the New York State Teachers Association, the New York State School Boards Association, the New York State Congress of Parents and Teachers, the New York State Association of District Superintendents, the New York State Council of City and Village Superintendents, the New York State Association of Elementary School Principals, the Public Education Association, and the New York State Citizens Committee for the Public Schools.

Any member of the Conference Board may bring before it an educational problem or project for discussion by all members. If all are agreed that a given program is desirable and sound, the Conference Board sponsors it by gathering significant facts, promoting research, and publishing the results for use in the promotion of programs for the improvement of education. The Conference Board has been instrumental in securing funds for research and sponsoring research basic to state-wide educational need. This has been true, to a marked degree, in the study of state aid for education and in determining the amount of state aid to local districts.

The strength of the Conference Board is largely due to the fact that it provides a clearinghouse for educational ideas and seeks to bring about united effort for common causes. It coordinates action and utilizes to good advantage the leadership residing in the organizations of which it is comprised. Through constructive approaches to the solution of complex educational problems, an action program and an inservice program become one and the same.

*Instructional Improvement*

The supervisory staff in each Florida county school system annually files a statement of plans with the State Department of Education for the improvement of instruction during the current school year. Members of the State Department of Education study these plans and then meet with the local supervisory staff to consider possibilities for strengthening and improving them. The State Department of Education in Florida—as other state departments do—publishes a considerable number of inservice periodicals and bulletins.

*Joint Conferences*

"Operation Bootstrap" is the descriptive title of a series of conferences in Georgia in which superintendents have opportunity to hear outstanding speakers from all over the nation. The State Department of Education, the Georgia Association of School Superintendents, and the University of Georgia work together in developing and supporting these conferences. Funds to defray the expenses of the visiting consultants are provided by the State Board of Education. The director of the Division of Surveys and Field Studies at the University of Georgia serves as conference coordinator. Each conference in the series opens with a dinner meeting, followed by a session in which professional staff members of the State Department of Education bring superintendents up to date on new policies of the State Board of Education, new legislation, plans, and programs sponsored by the State Department of Education.

The second day of the conference is devoted to discussion of problems of special interest to superintendents. At the evening session, a well-informed educational leader from outside the state, who has had rich experience in school administration, addresses the group and participates in a question-and-answer period. The morning session of the third day is again devoted to specific problems of special concern to administrators. The conference closes with a luncheon meeting that day. Of the 198 system superintendents in the state, 113 participated in the first of these conferences, and 80 registered for credit at the University of Georgia.

## Cooperative Approaches

Each summer, young administrators come together at the University of Illinois for a period of six weeks to study school administration as it functions in local school systems. Leaders in the field of school administration, including those engaged in the preparation of administrators and those who are practicing administrators, serve as consultants and provide the leadership in this inservice program.

Northwestern University and the University of Chicago have instituted programs for practicing administrators. Some compensation for special assistantships and staff assignments aid school administrators with limited funds in meeting the cost of participation in the conferences. The State Department of Education encourages school boards to release administrators for a year's study. Leaders in the Illinois Association of School Boards have lent their support to these programs by encouraging school boards to assume some responsibility for financial assistance to practicing administrators who return to a university campus for study. So far, only a few school districts have provided financial assistance in the form of sabbaticals and partial or full salary. However, there is some evidence that more and more school board leaders are seriously considering such support for the improvement of school administration.

The State Department of Education in Illinois has taken the initiative in creating a council on educational research. One of the big over-all problems this council is considering is inservice education for school administration. The Illinois Education Association has agreed to conduct four or five drive-in conferences on this problem.

*Study Councils*

The State Department of Education in Tennessee works closely with four study councils. Listed in the order of their origin, they are councils for school superintendents, principals, system-wide supervisors, and local attendance teachers. Each council is designed for cooperative problem study by people with similar jobs and some common problems. For example, superintendents continuously study the Tennessee legal structure for public schools, local curriculum and instruction, and pupil transportation. Principals in past years have studied optimum age for school entrance, dropouts, and the improvement of reading. Supervisors have studied classroom visitation, and attendance teachers have studied the cause of dropouts. These are but illustrations of the focal points of interest of the work of these four councils.

Membership in the councils is not restricted. Every public school person in Tennessee who is in the group named by the council's title is a member. For example, every superintendent is considered to be a member of the Superintendents Study Council and every principal a member of the Principals Study Council. Although participation is voluntary, all superintendents and most persons in other categories are active participants.

The organization of the councils is simple. For example, there are no initiation fees, no membership cards, no dues, and no letterhead stationery bearing the organization's name. Each council has its elected chairman, its elected State Steering Committee, and its various work committees. And, except for the Principals Study Council, each is designed to have a full membership meeting once a year. Each council is sponsored by the State Department of Education. Sponsorship provides (a) consultants as needed from the Department or from elsewhere, (b) executive secretarial services by a member of the State Department, (c) travel expenses for the meeting of the State Steering Committee, and (d) travel expenses for the over-all annual meeting. Sponsorship does not bring control from the State Department, for each council selects its own problems for study, conducts its study as it sees fit, and decides what it will include in its report.

Each council gathers facts and compiles the information needed in its work through small committees. These committees usually find the information they need in the reported practices and published findings of individual research workers and school systems. Sometimes, however, a council finds it necessary to collect its own information firsthand.

A good illustration of this latter approach is seen in a current study of the Superintendents Study Council. This study grew out of a question which Tennessee newspapers, speakers, some school people, and others kept raising insistently: Are schools spending too much time on athletics and other extracurricular activities and not enough time on classroom instruction?

This was obviously a question of *judgment*, and in order to provide an *objective* basis for answering it, the Council investigated several factual questions: During the school day, how much time do pupils actually devote to attending classes, preparing for classes, and participating in athletics? Outside the school day, how do they distribute their time among school-related activities? Similar questions were raised for teachers and for principals.

This study developed in the following manner: A committee of the Council prepared a proposed design of the investigation. It received consultative services from the State Department of Education and from Tennessee colleges and universities. The Council's State Steering Committee approved the study design. The State Department of Education provided special IBM cards, data processing personnel, and machines. Local school personnel, acting in each system under the direction of its own superintendent, made a one-year trial run to test the study instruments. The next year the actual study data were collected.

The people in Tennessee now have a factual basis for judging how well public school people are using their school time. But even more important than the data, the study council idea is helping them develop a clearer understanding of the problems and issues confronting the schools in the state of Tennessee and is providing an objective basis for forming opinions and making decisions.

*Curriculum Development*

The Oregon State Department of Education operates a series of workshops to strengthen administrative leadership in curriculum development. These are five-day sessions held at remote locations away from usual distractions. Well-versed authorities in educational administration and curriculum are employed by the Department to work with its own members in providing consultant services in the workshops. Since 1957, five state-level workshops and two regional workshops have been held. The purposes of these workshops are to help school administrators understand the reasons for curriculum revision and to give them the understandings and skills necessary for initiating and carrying out local curriculum development programs. These administrative workshops in curriculum are conducted as one phase of Oregon's $80,000 per-year state curriculum improvement program. Under this program, $60,000 per year is earmarked for assistance to local school districts carrying on curriculum improvement programs, and $20,000 is reserved for state-level curriculum improvement projects such as the institutes described above.

## School-Plant Planning

The Oregon School Board Association and the Oregon Association of School Administrators have cooperated in a series of school-plant planning conferences over a period of eight years. The purpose of these conferences is to keep people who are primarily responsible for school-plant planning abreast of the latest developments in design, building materials, lighting, heating, ventilation, space utilization, and construction.

## County and Intercounty Programs

There are numerous programs organized and operated in counties and in areas of states comprised of several counties that are closer to local school boards and administrators than state and regional inservice programs. Here, only a few examples of such programs can be called to attention as illustrative examples.

## A Seven-County Program

The Southwest Michigan Association of School Administrators has a membership of approximately 100 county and local administrators and university professors of education in a seven-county area. Each year, this association sponsors 12 monthly meetings and two workshops. It has several committees working on specific school issues. The programs for the monthly afternoon meetings focus attention primarily on curriculum development and spotlight outstanding programs in the area. Presentations and discussions deal with such specifics as new concepts in guidance, community communications, school publications, teaching machines, specifications for purchasing, bidding practices, certification of administrators, and the power structure in local communities.

The fall workshop held at the Michigan Education Camp on St. Mary's Lake is a two-day conference attended by 250 administrators. The winter workshop, held at the Kellogg Center on the Michigan State University campus, is open to administrators from other regions and has a regular attendance of about 500.

An organization known as the "Minute Men" is maintained by the Association. It is on the alert to assist in quick communications by telephone throughout the seven-county area on any emergency educational problem that needs the immediate attention of all members.

## A County Program

The School Boards Association of Calhoun County, Michigan, is a working organization which holds five regular meetings each year and has a membership of more than 100 representatives from the 42 rural and the 10 city and consolidated districts in the county. At the beginning of the school year, training sessions are planned for beginning board members. Programs for the five dinner meetings are planned around current topics of interest and are again primarily focused on the school board member's responsibility for curriculum development.

The Calhoun County organization of school administrators meets monthly. Officials of the county health department and state legislators from the county are members of the Association. In a series of meetings during a year, attention was given to the superintendent's role in curriculum revision, services of the State Department of Public Instruction, school legislation, and procedures for handling school funds. This group has been instrumental in the establishment of a county-wide educational program that brings special educational services to every child within the county who has need for such services. Considerable progress has been made through this association in cooperative purchasing, joint district use of staff specialists, and shared audiovisual libraries. Programs are developed by a committee which represents the membership of the Association. The county superintendent of schools serves as executive secretary for the group.

## Local School Districts

Although there is a great variation in depth and breadth, inservice programs for administrators and school board members are common in local districts. Most larger city districts have extensive programs within their own units and participate widely in inservice programs at national, state, and regional levels. Smaller school systems generally depend on programs planned outside the local district.

## Smaller Districts

Inservice programs for administrators in small districts may include—

1. Attendance at national, state, and regional meetings and workshops. Generally, the total cost of registration, travel, and subsistence is paid by the district.
2. Credit courses offered by institutions of higher learning either on campus or at extension centers. Many school districts partially subsidize or even pay the total costs of such study, though, sometimes administrators pay registration fees for credit courses if the credit is used in meeting requirements for an advanced degree.
3. Use of outside consultants. During recent years, a considerable number of consultant firms have been formed. Smaller school districts, as well as larger school systems, use the services of these firms. State governmental agencies and many tax-supported institutions of higher education offer such services on a no-fee basis, but, due to the increase in demand and the lack of funds to meet the demand, an increasing number of colleges and universities are being forced to charge for consultant services.
4. Subscriptions to magazines, bulletins, and other publications. Sometimes, such publications are purchased with school district funds, but in many instances, they are paid for by the superintendent himself and regarded as an investment in his own professional growth.

## Larger Districts

The range, intensity, and complexity of administrative problems in a large school system, particularly in a large city district, necessitate continuous programs of research, curriculum development, financial planning, evaluation, site procurement, and school-plant construction. There is scarcely any time in the year in which school board members, teachers, and members of the superintendent's headquarters staff, together with the superintendent and lay citizens of the community, are not deeply involved in seeking solutions to such overriding problems of school administration. As new information is developed, new insights are obtained, and workable solutions to problems are found, inservice growth on the part of everyone involved inevitably takes place. But over and above these workaday activities, most large school systems have developed inservice programs through which new perspectives to the problems and issues that confront the school system are sought and leadership potential increased.

*Graduate study.* In 1954, the Flint Graduate Center for Community School Leadership was organized in conjunction with Eastern Michigan University. The purpose of this program is to prepare educational leaders. The community is used as an experience laboratory. Administrators in the Flint school system are required to enroll in this program, which may lead to the M.A. degree at Eastern Michigan or to the six-year degree at Michigan State University. This program is now open to people outside Flint and attracts 400 to 500 enrollees each semester. Sessions for the Flint administrators are held in the morning and evening. Week-end sessions are scheduled for students who come from other school systems.

*Business, industry, and education.* The Leadership Training Seminar, sponsored in cooperation with the University of Chicago Industrial Relations Center, is another inservice program that is operated in the Flint school system. This program enrolled 120 school administrators and the same number of Flint business and industrial administrators. Spread over three semesters, this seminar covers leadership techniques, communication skills, and management-employee relations for business, industry, and education.

*A doctoral program.* Chicago has initiated a program for administrators which may be considered both inservice and preservice. It is so termed because administrators on the job, as well as individuals preparing for administrative positions, may enroll. This administrative internship program is a cooperative project supported by universities in the area and the Chicago public schools. It is a part of a two-year doctoral program in which the candidate spends one year at a university and one year as an intern with a principal or with a district assistant or associate superintendent who directs his field activities. Admission into the program is based on careful screening of applicants, with special attention given to traits, aptitudes, philosophical points of view, and capabilities deemed essential for success as an administrator and a doctoral student.

*District superintendents and principals.* The district superintendents in Chicago are providing the leadership for and giving direction to inservice education for men and women already employed as school administrators in the city system. There are 20 district superintendents, each of whom has under his supervision 20 or 30 principals of elementary and secondary schools. In each of the 20 districts, study groups and committees of principals work on projects growing out of needs in the district. Teachers, subject consultants, central office service personnel, and university faculty members serve as resource people. In every instance, research is carried on to determine the nature and extent of need. On the basis of the data gathered and wide reading, suggestions and recommendations for action are made. When the work on a district project has been completed, a report is made to the entire district personnel. Often, the reports are presented in pamphlet form and made available to all other districts.[8]

### Viewed in Entirety

This overview of inservice programs for school administration in this country which, of necessity, is incomplete, spotty, and little more than a sampling, gives an impression of the widely spread interest and great involvement of institutions, governmental agencies, professional organizations, and individual administrators in inservice activities of one kind or another. Clearly, there is a tremendous range and variety of programs under way. Nearly everything than can be thought of or imagined that has implications for improving school administration and for making the schools better is being tried somewhere in some degree and in some fashion. Programs range all the way from high-level, concentrated seminars involving carefully selected people over a period of several weeks to informal evening meetings of administrators and school board members in which procedures for purchasing school supplies are discussed.

Educational leaders in institutions of higher education, chief state school officers, executive secretaries of state education associations, and leaders of state associations of school administrators and school boards have provided much of the initiative for getting local, state, and regional inservice programs under way. Financial support from foundations has been an important factor in critical initial stages.

From this overview, one gets the impression of a ferment, of a stirring, of something in the making with more promise than accomplishment. Administrators and school boards are groping for deeper insights and clearer vision. The growing importance of education in the total life of the nation and the urgencies of the times have made them feel a deeper sense of responsibility for giving direction to the educational pro-

---

[8] Sclareb, Lester J., associate superintendent of schools, Chicago, Illinois. In response to the Commission's inquiry.

gram and for shaping the institution of public education. There is an eagerness to do something more and something better in small districts as well as in larger city systems. The growing complexity of nearly everything in and about the school, from the heating and ventilating system in a high school plant to the instructional program in the physical sciences, has compounded the problems that confront them.

Inservice programs have developed in response to the growing need for assistance. Immediate interest and a feeling that anything which can be done is better than nothing seems to have been the motivating force that gave impetus to many of the programs. Long-range, careful planning is the exception rather than the rule. One looks in vain for a continuous thread of purpose running through the multiplicity of in-service activities in a state or a region. Programs are built on top of programs in some localities, while in other localities there is little or nothing. Financial support is meager, and the resources that are available may not always be used to best advantage. Trial and error rather than adherence to tried and proven principles and movement toward well-established goals characterizes these widespread activities.

Roughly, these programs can be seen in four general categories.

1.  There is much participation in meetings, conferences, and work-shops held outside local districts. These inservice activities range in duration from a one-day session to workshops extending over a period of several weeks. They are sponsored and directed for the most part by professional associations, by colleges and universities, and by state educational agencies.

2.  Many administrators are enrolled in credit courses offered on the campuses of institutions of higher education or at extension centers established within driving distance of the local school systems from which the administrators come. Some districts are providing inservice education opportunities through sabbatical leaves wherein all or part of the individual administrator's salary continues to be paid while he is on the campus of a university as a student or is in an intern status. Many districts pay part of the cost and some pay all of the cost of credit courses taken by administrators in their school systems.

3.  Consultative services in some form are used by an increasing number of school districts. State educational agencies have traditionally provided consultative services. There are indications now that the rapidly increasing demand for assistance with problems of school administration has overtaxed the budgetary appropriations and staff available in state departments. Consequently, districts are turning to other sources for help. Many state universities provide consultative services, quite frequently on a fee basis. Such charges by tax-supported institutions indicate that, by and large, inservice

education is not regarded as a responsibility of the institutions of higher education, at least to the extent that essential budgetary appropriations for its support are provided. It continues to be thought of, to a great degree, as a responsibility of the individual. But the growing number of local districts which are contributing to the cost of inservice programs clearly indicates an increasing sense of responsibility on the part of local school systems for improving administrative leadership. Private consultant firms are being used more frequently to make surveys and to make recommendations for dealing with a wide variety of educational problems. Many of these consultant firms have very capable people and unquestionably supply high-quality service. In other instances, people who are not well informed and who are not sensitive to the intricate character and qualities of a community educational program give quick and neatly packaged answers to difficult problems.

4. A growing number of inservice publications is available. It can almost be said that no national or state organization or no well-recognized institution is without its publications department. Professional libraries in local school districts and in individual schools are growing rapidly.

This overview of an inservice program, despite all that is being done, indicates that only a small number of school systems and superintendents are being reached with worthwhile programs. For the most part, it is the stronger school systems that are served best. The problem is how to interest administrators and boards of education who have no awareness that they are failing the children of their community to seek help and to use help when it is available. Without awareness of the needs that exist in their school districts and without a deep-seated desire to do something better than is now being done in the way of providing an educational program for a generation of children and youth, there is no motivation for improvement or reason to turn to an inservice program.

# CHAPTER SEVEN

# The Role of the
# Local School Board

CREATING, supporting, and operating a system of public education that is open to everybody and that stands ready to serve everybody is a function of government that is as well established in this country as is the responsibility for safeguarding the rights and privileges of individual citizens. The prime purpose underlying this firmly fixed public responsibility for education is not to give advantages to individuals, but to undergird, to sustain, and to strengthen the processes of free government—in short, to make democracy work. In school government, as indeed in every other branch of government, the common good—the welfare of the state and nation and of society as a whole—is best served by developing as nearly as possible the full potential of each and every individual.

It is upon this fundamental principle that public taxation for the support of schools, compulsory school attendance laws, and legislative measures to safeguard the lives and well-being of each and every occupant of the school are based. The Land Ordinance of 1787 declares that "religion, morality, and knowledge, being necessary to good government and the happiness of mankind, schools and education shall be forever encouraged." It is in this sense, and in keeping with this fundamental principle of government, that public education has been firmly established as a responsibility of state government. It is in this sense that state school systems have been created and local school boards established as state agencies.

School boards are endowed with broad discretionary powers. The manner in which these powers are exercised goes far in shaping the character and the quality of the educational program and the opportunities that are available to children and youth and, in growing measure, to more mature citizens. The school board is close to the people; it is easy to believe that it enjoys a fuller measure of confidence than any other governmental agency. A survey made by the American Association of School Administrators in 1962, in which responses were received from 6,111 school superintendents, shows that 9 out of every 10 board members are elected by the people.

The typical citizen, particularly in the smaller school system, regards the school board member as a neighbor who has been chosen by those who know him best to transmit their concerns and interests on educational matters into policy that gives direction to the community's educational program. In large measure, the parents of the school district have entrusted the educational future of their children to these board members. The school board is ultimately responsible for everything that is done in and about the schools. The actions it takes or fails to take are reflected in the quality of teaching, the character of plants, the breadth of offerings, the allocation of funds, and, indeed, that inner spirit which in better school systems can be readily observed in the vigor, enthusiasm, confidence, and the satisfaction of accomplishments in the work of everyone in and about the schools.

The school board does not perform its functions merely by sitting and waiting. It makes decisions related to pertinent problems and issues, pursues courses that in its best judgment lead most directly to the broad purposes of the educational program, and initiates action wherever in its best judgment the results can be most fruitful. If it keeps full faith with the confidence the people of the community have placed in it, the school board is forever striving to improve the quality of the instructional program. It may seek this end at times by taking action to modify teacher-pupil ratios, by adjusting salary schedules, or by providing for new and better types of instructional tools and equipment. In other instances, the school board may decide that the most progress can be made by stimulating and supporting an inservice program that will strengthen and improve the administrative leadership in the school district. Such has been the case in many examples pointed out in Chapter 6 of this publication, in which a wide variety of inservice educational programs have been instituted.

In the allocation of school district resources, alternatives are always weighed by every thoughtful board of education. In weighing these alternatives, the board has full responsibility for asking itself and others upon whom it depends for counsel and advice whether expenditures of time and effort made in an inservice program hold more promise for improving the instructional program for the students in the schools than expenditures used in some other manner.

This Commission on Inservice Education contends that every inservice program of any substantial proportion that draws upon school district resources—whether they be in the form of financial outlay or the use of staff time—should be undergirded by school board policy. Without such support, inservice programs, no matter how boldly conceived, will rest upon an unstable foundation and have little chance for notable and long success.

In assessing its responsibility for inservice education for its administrative staff, the local school board can reasonably assume the following:

*American public education must be further improved.* If the public education enterprise had "arrived," there would be no problem. There would only remain the relatively simple task of securing administrative leadership properly grounded in what should be done. True, the necessary facilities and equipment and an adequately motivated public and student body would still be required. But, if there is an imperative to re-examine the basic commitments of education to our society, if the public schools are to prepare people to deal with an explosion of knowledge and the burgeoning expectations of two-thirds of the world's population—if education is really to *educate*—then the local school board must gird itself for a new and an exciting challenge.

This will not be a simple task for local school boards. Traditionally, the only logical position for a school system to assume with its public seems to have been that it is adequately meeting the needs of its student body and its community. No very convincing rationale has been developed which permits a school district to make a major effort toward study and improvement of the educational program without the implication of serious shortcomings. In their "public relations" efforts, school district leaders have often unwisely convinced themselves of the adequacy of the program and have, in the process, closed the door to effective progress. School boards must begin with a serious examination of the fundamental assumption that a new house must be constructed upon the foundation of the old, without unduly disturbing the residents.

*Effective administrative leadership cannot be bought; it must be developed.* In school board literature, one frequently finds the statement that the school board's most important task is to employ a capable superintendent. It obviously follows that all administrative personnel should be carefully selected. But there is more to it than this. A board cannot select better administrators than there are. The best will continue to be attracted to the better paying positions and to positions in which opportunities for professional leadership appear to be greatest. As a matter of fact, many board members will complete their tenure on a board of education without ever being required to participate in the selection of a superintendent for their district.

But every board has continuous responsibility and many opportunities to provide a setting in which the administrative staff can become increasingly effective. At the risk of oversimplifying the problem, it is contended here that this requires only a structure in which the administration is expected and permitted to administer the affairs of the school system *and* a climate in which the individual staff members are expected and permitted to learn and grow.

The underlying purpose in the many examples of inservice programs cited in Chapter 6 strongly indicates that major emphasis in school administration is shifting from concern for control and management to concern for leadership. Unless this shift is incorporated in the concept boards of education have of administration, no administrative staff is likely to have either the time or the courage to involve itself in any serious program of inservice education. Controls, administrative procedures, and routines beget more controls, administrative procedures, and routines. The school board that desires its administrators to escape from the treadmill of managerial duties must itself believe that administration is leadership as well as management.

*School boards must accept broad responsibility for the improvement of educational administration.* School boards have been slow to commit the resources of their districts to upgrading school administration. Since personal growth and increased training often lead to changes in position, boards as a rule have tended to view investment in developing administrative leadership as a way to make schools better in stronger neighboring districts, but of little benefit to the schools in their own system. Inservice education for *teachers* is much more widely accepted; yet an examination of the tenure of staff personnel would probably reveal that administrators serve the same district as long as or longer than classroom teachers. As a matter of fact, superintendents change positions less often than is commonly believed. The 1962 study of AASA membership showed that of the 6,111 members specifically identified as school superintendents, almost half had served in only one district; and 72 percent, or approximately three-fourths, had served as superintendents in only two districts.

The soundest and perhaps the most economical step local school boards can take toward improving the educational program in their own districts is to make administrative positions more attractive. Almost every school district in the nation could do much more than it is now doing to upgrade the educational program by giving substantial support to inservice education for school administration. A school system that attracts and holds outstanding administrative leadership already is or soon becomes an outstanding school system. Obviously, local school district reorganization and substantial efforts by the state and national government to equalize the financial ability of school districts help. Over the past few years, much has been accomplished by these measures. But much more is needed. Wide disparities in educational leadership of school districts still exist; and, in large measure, this is reflected in the quality of educational programs. Much more effort should be directed toward removing the glaring deficiencies that exist and to strengthening the educational programs where there are deficiencies. "As is the teacher, so is the school" is an old maxim that perhaps would be equally true if restated, "As is administrative leadership, so is the school system."

While there undoubtedly is no one best approach to improving administrative leadership, the Commission suggests the following guidelines for boards of education which strive to make inservice education for school administration a reality:

*It is essential that an adequate local administrative organization be developed.* School administration has unjustly suffered from the contention that it does not "produce" anything. Such criticism is directed, in particular, at personnel whose assignment is to serve those who carry on the instructional task. Where they exist, such impressions can be attributed more often to understaffing than to overstaffing. It is an empty exercise to discuss the inservice education of an administrative team which is understaffed or which is not adequately provided with clerical help, office space, equipment, and the like. A cooperative study by board and superintendent of the school district's administrative organizational needs for services to support classroom teaching and staff utilization might pay handsome dividends in improved operation and performance in all aspects of administration.

*All administrative personnel should be employed for the full year.* Superintendents and certain other central office personnel are usually employed on a year-round basis. Other members of the administrative staff—principals, supervisors, and consultants—are released each summer to swell the labor supply or to pursue an occasional course of study. There is, in effect, an unused supply of "professional manpower." If these people were employed on a year-round basis, they could lighten the load of the chief administrator so that he would have time for professional study, and they, in turn, would have time to work in an inservice program. Most school administrators are resourceful enough—given the blessing of the board of education—to apportion the administrative task so that all can be involved in an inservice education program.

*Boards should provide financial assistance for programs of study which require extended leaves of absence by administrators.* In addition to the problem of an adequate replacement during a temporary absence, most school administrators have personal responsibilities which make it difficult, if not impossible, to live for long without a regular salary. School boards should seriously consider adopting a policy for administrators which would permit half salary for approved full-time leaves of absence or three-quarter salary for approved half-time leaves of absence, or some variation of such a formula. Where state laws make such a procedure questionable, efforts should be made to enact legislation to legalize it.

*Board policy should provide for participation of administrators in a broad pattern of professional activities.* Obviously, a simple way for a board to encourage its superintendent and other administrators in the school system to join with other leaders in the profession in studying educational problems and long-range planning is to provide an ample budget for it. This budgetary allocation, the same as all other items in the budget, should be administered by the superintendent. The board's expressed interest in the participation of its administrative staff in professional activities and its encouragement of the staff to contribute to the work of their profession are of equal importance.

*School boards should make use of consultants and resource people from outside the district in assessing their problems and developing programs for improvement.* Almost every school district is within reach of an institution of higher education which has some degree of interest in the improvement of elementary and secondary education. Here, again, the wise board of education will appropriate funds, perhaps modest at the beginning, specifically designated for such purposes. The extreme provincialism of some local districts might be lessened if university staff members could be induced to conduct, in cooperation with local school systems, regional studies encompassing several school districts. The possibilities here for the improvement of school administration seem almost unlimited, but little more than a beginning has been made.

A note of encouragement to boards of education and some simple suggestions of first steps to take were succinctly expressed by the American Association of School Administrators in its 1960 Yearbook:

Boards can aid an administrator's inservice growth by approving adequate budgets for professional meetings, in-school consultants, and current books and journals. From board members, too, the alert administrator gets cues for new ideas, experimentation, and even new areas for his own study. The complete role of boards in the area of inservice education has yet to be spelled out as fully as it should be, but the recent acceleration of board association activity predicts better days ahead.[1]

While the role of the school boards has not yet been well defined, the idea of school boards' participating actively in inservice education for school administration is catching on. The Commission strongly encourages school board associations and their member boards throughout the land to join with professional associations of administrators, with state departments of education, and with colleges and universities in this movement.

## Inservice Education for School Board Members

By no means everything that needs to be done to improve and strengthen school administration can be accomplished, even through well-conceived and well-executed inservice programs for school superintendents and other professional staff members. The board of education carries heavy responsibilities; much depends upon what it does; and for this reason, if for no other, the board itself should seriously engage in an inservice program designed to bring clearer vision and better understanding to bear on shaping policy and to give direction to the total educational program.

The American school board has served over the years the important purpose of keeping the public schools responsive to the will of the people. Because of its nearness to the people and because of its considerate action, it has made the schools truly of the people rather than creatures of general government, professional educators, or private corporations. The board has successfully protected the public schools against the domination of any special ism or centralized movement for remolding society. The schools in this country began as local institutions. School boards have kept them that way.

The school in any district at any given moment in large measure is a result of what has happened in the past. It has been built out of the

[1] National Education Association, American Association of School Administrators. *Professional Administrators for America's Schools.* 1960 Yearbook. Washington, D.C.: the Department. 1960 pp 196-97

thoughts, hopes, aspirations, and actions of the people. In assuming its responsibilities, the school board, in effect, becomes an inheritor of all that has happened in the past. It accepts the school or the school system, as the case may be, with all of its strengths and weaknesses, with all of its accomplishments and failures, with all of its problems and needs, and with all of its traditions and standards of practice. Whatever is accomplished in the way of improvement must be made by moving forward. No board of education can turn the clock backward.

The school board's most important responsibility is for what the school will become. The statement so often made that the school board acts for the people but does not think for the people disposes of an important administrative relationship in terms that are too neatly phrased to be entirely accurate. The school board that quietly waits for a mandate from the people before it acts has relinquished its leadership. Instead of leading it is being pushed and driven or is drifting with the currents of community pressures. The school board that meets its full responsibilities to the people it serves stimulates people to look toward the future, encourages long-term planning, and initiates action that will lead to school improvement. If the school board will not think for the people, then it must accept responsibility for getting the people to think for themselves.[2]

It is toward the end of meeting broad responsibilities that the inservice program for school board members should be directed. To begin with, it is essential that school boards be made up of able persons—persons who have the integrity to stand for their own convictions; persons who have the courage to withstand the pressures of narrow, selfish interests; persons who treat the interests and concerns of the citizen in the most lowly position in the community with the same degree of respect and consideration as the sentiments of the most highly regarded citizen; and, above all, persons who are fully and conscientiously committed to making the schools strong enough to be effective in meeting the needs of all children and youth in the district.

Selection of personnel for boards of education is probably as important as the selection of administrative personnel, for the best superintendent is seriously handicapped and has but little chance for success with a board that operates with shortsighted and ill-conceived policy. Not only citizens of the community but boards as well have a responsibility for encouraging highly qualified individuals to become candidates for school boards. While "self-perpetuation" of boards should not be encouraged, boards can properly be interested in the continuation of an orderly and constructive approach to the solutions of problems in a school district. They cannot escape their responsibilities for keeping the

[2] Cooper, Shirley, and Fitzwater, Charles O. *County School Administration.* New York: Harper & Brothers, 1954. pp. 355-56.

community informed of proposed solutions to immediate and long-range educational problems and, at the same time, for assisting the electorate in securing capable citizens for the important duties of school board membership.

Means through which the people of the school district may have an opportunity to select candidates who are familiar with the issues facing public education and with the objectives of the schools are a matter of prime consideration for the board of education. Certainly, the board should assist a community in developing practices by which qualified and open-minded citizens become candidates for the board. Once such a procedure has been developed, the board should identify itself with the plan and should use its considerable influence to discourage the election of self-seeking individuals or those who represent dissident elements.

Democracy is not necessarily served by the opportunity to choose between two or more individuals for a seat on a board of education if none of the candidates is capable. It can be served if at least one candidate exists who, by background of experience and familiarity with local problems, is prepared to become a contributing member of a policy-making group for a local school system. The growing practice of setting up caucuses or nominating committees to select and endorse candidates for boards of education has promise for improving school board membership and performance.

The good school board member is committed to learning and growing. According to legend, Athena sprang full grown and fully armed from the head of her father, Zeus. Good board members do not come into being with the abruptness of this famed Greek goddess. The process of election or appointment to a board does not automatically convert even the most highly respected citizen into an effective member.

It is a serious fallacy to assume that, because a board of education is composed of laymen, the members can be excused for being uninformed regarding the fundamental issues with which they will deal. If American public education is to function under the direction of thousands of local school boards, it seems obvious that its long-term accomplishments will depend, in large measure, upon the sum total of the understanding of such boards. Someone has said that art is as demanding of its audience as it is of its creator. In somewhat comparable manner, one might say that public education in America is as demanding of its citizens and their chosen representatives as it is of its professional leaders and the students whom they serve. This is at once a challenge and an overriding problem of democracy in action.

How, then, shall a board of education get hold of its task? The generally accepted distinction between the function of a board of education and the function of a superintendent is that the board establishes policy and the superintendent administers it. This is perhaps an oversimplification of a most important relationship. However, boards and administrators work out an arrangement through which boards can carry out their responsibilities without making too many decisions of an administrative nature, and procedures can be developed so that a board can comfortably leave the administration of the school system to the superintendent and his staff. Such an approach releases time and energy which the board may use to good advantage in its own improvement.

Public education is confronted with tremendous challenges—challenges of crucial importance not only to the people in the local district where a particular school is located but to the entire country. Boards of education and administrators must more fully comprehend the full dimensions of these challenges and their implications for policy and decisive action. The problem is to see the educational program in its totality rather than as a cluster of details and specifics. Edward M. Tuttle, the first secretary of the National School Boards Association, has said that boards of education are not aiming high enough in their hopes or in their work for the schools. They should devote some portion of their deliberations to a discussion of what schools (not necessarily their schools) should be trying to do. And they must seek to understand the place of public education in the shape of things to come.

It is equally essential that boards of education see their problems and relate their decisions and actions to the legal, financial, and social structure within which the schools operate. Too often, local school boards accept as absolutes an archaic district organization, an inadequate tax structure for the support of schools, and an outdated posture on the part of the community toward the task of the schools. These overriding problems call for careful study and deliberate rather than hasty action on the part of school boards. Usually, effective action will have to be taken by some other governmental agency or at points outside the legal jurisdiction of the board. However, it is the nature of a representative democracy that legislative action usually follows rather than precedes understanding on the part of the citizenry. Boards of education can and do in many instances play a strategic role in developing the necessary understanding for effective democratic action on broad educational problems.

No blueprint is here proposed for the inservice education of school board members. However, there is no hesitancy on the part of the Commission in encouraging and, if need be, urging that superintendents and boards develop an inservice program designed to orient new board members to the position of community trust they have accepted and to stimulate study of the objectives and plans of the school district on the part of all members. The school administration and the staff of a school system stand to profit equally with board members from such a carefully developed program of study. While it is desirable for a school board to be conversant with what goes on in a school system, it is proposed that this kind of inservice education must be more than how-to-do-it sessions in which members of the profession describe their work, and their listeners try to decide whether or not they would do it that way. Study should precede action on all important matters. Intelligent action may be expected to follow understanding. To separate study and action at the local level will require real statesmanship on the part of the leadership of the board and of the superintendent. If state and national associations of school boards were to embrace this concept and reflect it in projections of inservice programs for school board members at the district level, it would be extremely encouraging.

Inservice education of school board members should be a major objective of state, regional, and national associations of school boards. The National School Boards Association is taking a strong lead in moving toward this objective. In a recent publication, the Association states the following:

The National School Boards Association works at the national level as an affiliation of all fifty states and territorial associations, assisting them to meet their mutually shared objectives, and undertaking service and informational activities for broad, national purposes of educational improvement which the individual associations, working separately, are not organized to undertake. The NSBA is dedicated to increasing public understanding of the importance of school board service to America's public education and to the American way of life. It is pledged to work for the general advancement of education for the youth of the United States and its possessions. It works for the most efficient and effective organization and administration of the public schools.[3]

Most school board members in the nation are perhaps unaware of these purposes. Nevertheless, this national association of school boards stands committed to improving the quality of public education by increasing the understanding of school board members. It is hoped that the leadership of the Association will strive to implement this objective and that both lay and professional leaders in education throughout the land will support them in this extremely important effort.

---

[3] National School Boards Association. *You and the NSBA—Quality Schools Through Quality Boards.* Chicago: the Association, 1959. pp. 3-4.

In a manner comparable to the action taken by the National School Boards Association, state associations of school board members are accepting responsibility for inservice education of their membership. The following excerpt from the Constitution of the Illinois Association of School Boards is a good illustration:

> The object of the Association is the constant improvement of public school education in the State of Illinois.
> For the accomplishment of this object, the Association shall, among other things:
>
> a. Study educational problems.
> b. Inform school boards of the results of its studies, advise school boards of sound educational policies and practices, and encourage their adoption.
> c. Furnish the general assembly with information pertaining to educational legislation.
> d. Cooperate with public officers, school administrators and teachers and with interested organizations in advancing the cause of public education in this state.

These concisely stated purposes clearly show that the men and women who founded this organization wished not only to permit but also to encourage widespread study on the part of school boards. Undoubtedly, the constitutions of other state associations have a similar orientation. But a statement of purpose and a declaration of intention are not enough. They must be followed up with a never-ending program of action—a program of action that requires statesmanlike leadership, persistent effort, and firm commitment to an important purpose. State-wide organizations made up of boards of education with a continuously changing lay membership are hard put to launch and to sustain a study program that has depth and breadth.

White's study of the school boards in 3,950 districts with an enrollment of more than 1,200 pupils shows that 13.2 percent of the almost 24,000 members had been in office for less than a year; 40.2 percent had served 1 to 5 years; 30.1 percent had served 5 to 10 years; 13.7 percent had served 10 to 20 years; and 2.9 percent had served for 20 years or more. Of these 3,950 school boards, 52.4 percent had a member with less than one year's experience, and 88.9 percent had one or more members with from 1 to 5 years' experience.[4]

With the rapid turnover in school board membership that these data indicate, much of the time and effort expended in inservice programs will almost inevitably be required to orient incoming members to the status

[4] White, Alpheus L. *Local School Boards: Organization and Practices.* U.S. Office of Education, Bulletin No. 8. Washington, D.C.: Government Printing Office, 1962. pp. 32-33.

and operational procedures of local district boards. Moving the inservice program beyond this elementary stage to a point where board members have opportunities for depth study of the broad social and economic problems and the great issues that have a bearing on school board policy and action is a great task. Even if the professional staff of the state school boards association were adequate for launching a broadly conceived inservice program for school board members, they still would face the fact that the immediate needs and desires of local school boards would claim high priority in any inservice program projected. Most state school board leadership deserves high commendation for what has been accomplished. However, aid and encouragement from state departments of education and local school board leaders is desperately needed.

Organizations which have many purposes usually tend to disappoint people whose major concern is about only one of these purposes. This explains why operational structures with a single objective so frequently develop. The School Board Seminar in the Chicago suburban area is such a single-purpose organization. The original purpose of the seminar was to present material which would enable school boards to find realistic and genuine solutions to present-day school problems—to provide active and prospective board members, professional educators, and community leaders with a better understanding of school board functions and relationships in the local districts.

Here, through cooperative effort, a relatively small number of school boards located in close proximity to each other has moved ahead in a series of pilot seminars from which there is much reason for believing an extensive program will emerge for the education of veteran, new, and prospective school board members. While such an effort is admittedly in the pilot or exploratory stage, it may well have the dual advantage of localizing the program so that attendance can be solicited and, at the same time, of allowing the board member to leave his local setting where he is accustomed to a posture of commitment and decision making to see his responsibilities and problems in broader prospective.

The board of education is at the center of the deliberations and decisions that determine the direction in which public education will move and, to a considerable degree, how effective it will be. With this important role in educating the children and youth of the nation in one of the most crucial periods of its history, it seems to be beyond question that school boards should be made up of able persons and that inservice education of school board members should be a major objective of associations of school boards.

## Dealing in Futures

In this crucial historic period of rapid cultural change and world tensions that again and again seem strained almost to the breaking point, school boards in every district in the land are called upon to look to the future steadfastly and clearly. The policies they adopt are the bases for future action. The results of many of the most important decisions they make will not be fully realized for years to come. The community educational program for which they are so largely responsible deals in futures. Somehow, school boards, together with their superintendents and the teachers who work day after day with pupils in the classroom, must shape educational programs that will give a generation of children and youth the alertness, the self-confidence, the skills and understandings, the commitment to high purposes, and the creative powers needed in a world in which the frontier of today becomes commonplace tomorrow.

The greatest and by far the most important resource with which school boards work as they seek to shape an educational program to meet the challenges of the future is the professional staff of teachers and administrators in the school system. As teachers and administrators become more sensitive to the intricate processes through which children grow and learn, as they more fully understand the myriad forces that motivate their actions and shape their behavior, as they become more familiar with the processes of dynamic culture, and as their skills in organizing curriculum content and handling instructional methods are increased, new dimensions of quality will be added to the educational program. Constructing and equipping laboratories, increasing and improving library services, increasing budgets, procuring better school sites, extending transportation programs, revising teachers' salaries, and reshaping the organization for instruction—all will contribute in due course to the improvement of the instructional program. But in the final analysis, the greatest contribution to improving the schools of this country and to assuring a vitally alive school experience for every child will be made by adding to the strength and quality of the professional staff.

As school boards move to meet the challenges which confront them and, indeed, which confront the nation as a whole, they can and must see that an investment in the professional growth of their school superintendent and the people with whom he works is one of the surest, one of the most sensible, and one of the most economical ways of adding the new dimensions of quality to the educational program that everyone feels the schools must have.

# CHAPTER EIGHT

# The Role of the
# Institution of Higher Education

$O$VER the years, the distance between the institution of higher learning and business and industry; agriculture; local, state, and national government; and, indeed, the average citizen has decreased. The institution of higher learning does not stand apart from the ongoing life of the country. The problems of the people as they are faced in almost every field of endeavor become part of the content of the ongoing program of the institution of higher education. Faculty members serve again and again in consultative capacities as citizens work with problems of taxation, transportation, marketing and distributing the products of industry, and city planning. Laboratories have been established to conduct research where new information is needed. Institutes, conferences, and workshops have been set up to disseminate research findings and to bring them into practical use.

An examination of the charters and published literature of institutions of higher learning throughout the country reveals three areas to which these institutions profess commitment: teaching, research, and service. Teaching and research are areas of emphasis in practically all such institutions. Service is less common. Land-grant institutions are involved in service because of the very nature of the legislation that established them. The Agricultural Extension Service, which is, in effect, a working arm of land-grant institutions, has contributed materially to the development of agriculture by disseminating research findings and assisting farm people in putting them into practice. The surplus of food that at moments seems to embarrass this country is objective evidence of the success of this extensive service program.

The boundaries of the state are held to be the limits of the campus for a number of institutions of higher education. Such institutions have supported programs of adult education and general extension courses that have been successful. Many of these state programs have produced substantial results in the form of a more literate citizenry, a strengthened economic enterprise, higher standards of living, and better governmental services. Unfortunately, however, relatively few comprehensive programs of educational field services have been developed by colleges and universities.

Application of the general extension service concept to education can be justified in terms of the importance of education to the total well-being of the nation and the magnitude of the problems that confront the schools. Educational field service programs developed and operated by institutions of higher education can be expected to yield results equal to or greater than those obtained in the agricultural and industrial fields. The present conflict in the world and the accelerated tempo of cultural change have generated problems and created tensions wherein democracy must often operate in an atmosphere of urgency. Every citizen needs to be made aware of the many diverse problems that exist and the import of these problems. The growing amounts and kinds of information that people need to function well as citizens require a continuous program to apprise them of present-day problems and issues and of the outlook for the future. Just to convince the citizens of this country of this urgency is in itself a monumental task.

Institutions of higher learning are in a key position to furnish leadership in providing such services to society. Lack of leadership, leaving voids and frustrating uncertainties in place of clearly established goals and firm and resolute action, may well have led to the formation of the extremist groups which, though often well intentioned, may do more harm than good. It is the thesis here that institutions of higher education should and must take a hard look at their service function with a view to strengthening it. Administrators in institutions of higher education need to be convinced that the service aspect of their programs needs to be expanded. There is certainly no more fruitful place for this expansion to begin than through a carefully planned program of services to public education. Through serving the schools, the continuing education of the adult population can be strengthened and the vitality of our culture assimilated and made an integral part of the instructional program for elementary and secondary pupils.

Education in this present age is no longer finished with completion of the requirements for a high school diploma or a bachelor's degree. This is particularly true in a democratic society. All nations in the world are trying to raise their standards of living, and the first avenue to which they turn is education. While the leadership of this country in past years can be attributed in large part to a universal system of elementary and secondary education, this leadership can no longer be maintained at the level needed to cope with the problems of this complex age unless opportunities are extended to more people to continue their education throughout their lives. Education has been the means of resolving many problems of living; but, at the same time, it has added problems by making the culture more complex and making continuing education more necessary.

Universities that, by the nature of their organization and support, are strongly committed to serving agricultural and industrial enterprises through general extension services should likewise be committed to serving public education through a field service program. There is no justification for policy that supports agricultural and industrial enterprises and, at the same time, overlooks or neglects the public education endeavor. But the inservice program for school administration that is envisioned by this commission cannot be projected as a responsibility of land-grant institutions alone.

It is not too much to say that all institutions of higher learning which have major concern for the preparation of teachers and administrators and for conducting educational research have important contributions to make to an inservice program for school administration. Fortunately, institutions of higher learning are so distributed over the country that most school districts are in close proximity to a college or university. Faculty members in teacher-education institutions are sensitive to the unique problems and needs of nearby school systems. Each time a graduate of an institution is placed in a district as a teacher or an administrator, a vital link in communication between the institution and the operational program of the district has been established. Much of the material in the teacher-preparation program is drawn from these districts. While the financial support of inservice programs must and does come from different sources, private and public institutions alike are making important contributions to inservice programs, as has been pointed out again and again in Chapter 6 of this publication. These contributions need to be increased.

### Point of Beginning

No educational program in an institution of higher learning, whether it be of a preservice or an inservice nature or for graduate or undergraduate students, suddenly comes into being full blown and with full power. At the point of beginning, an inservice program for school administration is likely to be modest. There is opportunity for growth and much need for painstaking care in establishing a true course of direction.

Unless the administration of the institution is firmly convinced of the need for an inservice program; unless resources are mobilized, earmarked, and allocated; unless staff members are given the necessary assignments; and unless operational procedures are clearly established, the program will not be firmly grounded. Such development of basic policy is a crucial point in launching or expanding an inservice program. It is a point at which school administrators, local school board members, and citizens in the area served by the institution should join with faculty members in developing a clear understanding of the need for an inservice program, the scope of the services that will be provided, and the extent to which the services will be used. If a program is to have its full strength and vitality, it cannot be treated incidentally, regarded lightly, or considered as something that is merely tacked on. It must be developed as an essential and an integral part of the total program of the institution.

In the development of its inservice program for school administration, the institution must begin with what it has and then move forward. The point of beginning may be a general extension program in which some course work in school administration is offered at off-campus centers. It may be a series of institutes or conferences that are traditionally held on the campus. It may be a program of research and consultative services. It may be a contractual arrangement between the institution of higher education and a local school district in which assistance is given in carrying forward some aspect of the local district's program. It may be any one or all of these types of activities. Unless the institution is doing nothing at all in the way of field services—and this would be a rare instance—the inservice program will begin on the basis of what is already being done and move forward from existing operations.

As the program develops, it is reasonable to expect that the institution's field contacts with school districts will be strengthened, the work load of faculty members will be shifted so that more time and opportunity are provided for off-campus work, and more and more administrators and other educational leaders will join with faculty members in planning the program. Interdependence between the institution of higher education and local districts will increase, and a greater sense of unity will develop as ties are strengthened and the program expands.

In Washington State University, a beginning was made through the general extension division. Initial field contacts were made through regular meetings with school district faculties. The emphasis in these meetings was on improving the school district's educational program. University credit for the work done in these meetings was optional. The school district paid a fee to the extension division of the College of

Education sufficient to cover the cost of travel and subsistence for instructors and consultants. University staff members who were involved in these field activities were given teaching-load credit. Extra pay was not allowed.

Concurrently with these services to local school districts through the field service program, staff members were working with the state association of school administrators in providing assistance wherever possible. In the early stages of this relationship, the University's service to the association was limited largely to publication of newsletters, assistance with research on problems that concerned administrators, and the production of reports. As a result of these small ventures in an inservice program, the University became more sensitive to the needs of school districts and to the value of an inservice program; and, at the same time, accumulated some evidence that could be used in support of recommendations to the Board of Regents for a continuing and stronger service program. Eventually, field services to the schools, particularly in close proximity to the University, became an integral part of the program of the College of Education. This service program grew within a few years to the extent that the regular work load of four members of the staff included field services.

Financial support of the field service program is carried partly by the University through the allocation of staff time. Travel, subsistence, and incidental expenses incurred by the staff members in the field work are paid by the school districts receiving the service. Other members of the College of Education, as well as staff members from special fields in other divisions of the University, assist with the field service program on a voluntary basis. The manner and extent of the College of Education staff involvement in the inservice program varies considerably. One member gives three-fourths of his time to school plants and to citizen surveys, another member gives half of his time to a regional study council, another devotes half of his time to curriculum problems, and still another staff member spends three-fourths of his time in working on junior college problems. In addition to these people who have major responsibilities in the field service program, other staff members who are specialists in particular fields are available to make field trips when needed and are quite frequently called upon.

Graduate students are involved in this field service program and gain valuable experience through their field work. The entire staff feels that the field services program has improved the College of Education in all phases of its work—in teaching, in research, and in service. It has been especially helpful in keeping the University staff sensitive to the problems and needs in the day-to-day operations of the educational programs in the local districts. The essential elements in this successful attempt to develop a functional inservice program reside, in large part, in the attitudes of the administration and staff members of the College of Education. Foresight, as well as willingness to accept responsibility for improving education within the state, was basic to success of the program in its initial stages. The staff as a whole took a long-term point of view, holding to the objective that field work would, in the end, result in developing a larger and stronger graduate program and would give opportunities for actual experience to graduate students as well. Both of these objectives have been realized to a considerable extent.

### Value and Purpose

Value and purpose are the architects of the inservice program. They shape its organization, its content, and its design. The strength of the program lies, in large part, in the personal involvement of individuals, in the identity of their own interests and concerns with the program, in the opportunities it gives them to contribute ideas and viewpoints as well as to receive assistance, and in the ability and self-confidence it gives men and women to think for themselves and to act in an intelligent manner.

An inservice program will fall short of its highest purpose if it does not bring about changes in the understandings, in the attitudes, and in the behavior of people. Education at any level or in any form is a personal matter. It involves people in a most intimate way. If it is in keeping with the best-known principles of teaching and learning, it conveys meanings; it gives assistance at points where needs are felt; it changes thoughts, beliefs, and actions; it is uniquely adapted to the problems and interests of individuals and gives full consideration to the circumstances in which they live and work.

It is this personal involvement at every point in a well-conceived inservice program for school administration that makes cooperative planning so essential. Unless the institution of higher learning—in accepting the responsibility for providing an inservice program to a group of administrators, to the entire teaching staff in a school district, or to an entire community—fully understands the concerns, interests, and needs of the people whom it expects to serve, the program will have a superficial quality.

The inservice program should nowise disregard, disrupt, or violate the principles and methods of administrative organization and operation in the local district it serves. By law, by school board policy, by tradition, and by practice, responsibilities have been fixed, procedures have been established, and an intricate operation which involves board members, administrators, teachers, pupils, and lay citizens of the community has been developed. The inservice program should serve rather than seek to dominate this organization. It should fit into and become a part of this program rather than become an appendage. If recommendations for changes in procedures, changes in policies, or changes in the allocation of responsibilities should be made as a result of the inservice program, these changes should and must be brought about in the same orderly process within the limits of the school district's operational procedures as any other modifications in the program.

For the purposes of guiding the development and operation of an inservice program, four simple, understandable principles are called to attention here:

1. Equality of opportunity
2. Worth and dignity of the individual
3. Freedom of choice, freedom of initiative, and freedom of speech
4. Responsibility for self and for the general welfare.

It will be readily recognized that these are principles which were enunciated in the Declaration of Independence, the Preamble to the Constitution, the body of the Constitution where provisions are made for legislative and judicial systems, and the Bill of Rights. These principles are not mutually exclusive. They are interdependent. Freedom without responsibility would lead to anarchy or chaos, and without commonly accepted procedures for working together, the rights of individuals would be trampled upon and energy would be exhausted in bickering and strife. All who work from these principles must understand and accept all of them. They are the basis of human relations. They are fundamental to the democratic process. They must permeate all relationships and become personal convictions of all who work in the public schools and of all who assume responsibility for inservice programs.

## Human Relationships

As the university or any other institution or agency moves forward in developing an inservice program, it can scarcely do otherwise than to proceed on the assumption that the school administrator is an educational leader. His position in the school system places upon him leadership responsibilities that he must meet to some extent and in some manner— autocratically, democratically, or at some point between these extremes.

Directly and indirectly, his leadership reaches every member of the staff and permeates relationships in every segment and every aspect of school operation. The great challenge to the administrator is to make his leadership effective in his dealings with pupils and staff members and with lay citizens in the community. He should be as thoughtful and as considerate in his relationships with the youngest principal of a school, the newest teacher in the system, or the smallest child in a classroom as he is with members of the board. While all have different roles, each and every one is an individual clothed with a dignity that should not be violated or treated with indifference.

The leadership in an inservice program should be as considerate of individual personalities and as closely tuned to individual interests and needs as the leadership in the best-administered school system. If the inservice program in its own organization and operation cannot adhere to the principles of human relationships which it seeks to impart, it has failed at a crucial point.

### Policy, Rules, and Regulations

Without guiding policies and rules and regulations to give direction to an inservice program, time will be wasted, resources frittered away, efforts duplicated, and energies of people dissipated in frustrations that come from lack of clarity of purpose or well-defined roles. In a broadly conceived inservice program, there are likely to be two levels of policy and rules and regulations. There will be the policy for the over-all program which may be developed by the faculty of the institution of higher education, perhaps after some consultation with representative administrators from the school systems to be served; and there will be policies developed for the operation of specific programs in particular school districts. While there may be differences at many points, the policy statements that undergird the program in its totality and at specific operational points cannot be in conflict.

To clarify the meaning of policy and rules and regulations as intended here, a parallel can be drawn with policies and rules and regulations in a local school system. In the administration of a school system, a distinction must be made between policy and rules and regulations. Policies are statements or clearly defined positions which set forth purposes and prescribe, in general terms, the organization and the program of the school system. They express what is wanted. They indicate *why* and *how much*. They are general guides to action. Policies are usually written as declarative statements; that is, statements containing a positive or a revealing explanation of a condition. Specific directions telling *how, by whom, where,* and *when* functions are to be performed are commonly referred to as rules and regulations. Rules and regulations define or actually are the procedures for carrying out the details of administrative policy. Rules and regulations are written as imperative statements; they are directive. They designate procedures and courses to be followed in specific manner.

Policies for an inservice program for school administration are stronger, generally sounder, and serve their purposes to better advantage if the opinions, points of view, and interests of people who will be directly affected by their application have a voice in their formation. Action should not be hasty as beliefs, commitments, and information are gleaned from the varied experiences of informed and conscientious people and, in a sense, crystallized in policy statements. Once established and fully understood, policies should be carried out, until such time as changes are needed, without debate or controversy. To illustrate, the people of a village or a city may give serious consideration to the establishment of a system of traffic lights to regulate the movement of pedestrians and vehicles upon the streets. But once a system has been agreed upon and installed, it would be extremely confusing and hazardous for people to disregard the signals and debate the right-of-way at every street intersection.

Once the course of direction in an inservice program has been fully determined and the procedures for moving ahead well established, rules and regulations can be followed with decisiveness and without needless bickering over details.

### Fragmentation

People who are responsible for planning and operating an inservice program cannot overlook the fragmentation in the profession. There is a splintering into special interest groups wherever one looks. Elementary principals, secondary principals, classroom teachers, science teachers, mathematics teachers, and audiovisual instructors are organized into special groups. There is fragmentation among the administrators themselves. In some states, school administrators are organized into as many as three different groups. Comparable fragmentation is common in existing inservice programs. There are inservice activities in practically every subject-matter field and at every grade level in the elementary and secondary schools. There are programs for principals, for supervisors, for counselors, for school-lunch supervisors, for administrators of transportation, and for a whole array of specialists.

The superintendent of schools is so busily engaged in setting up inservice growth programs for other members of his staff, along with many other responsibilities he must meet, that he has little or no chance to consider seriously his own inadequacies and shortcomings and little time to give to his own professional improvement. From time to time, he goes to a university workshop or meeting with a selected group of superintendents for a day or a week end. At other times, he joins with superintendents of the first- or second-class school districts in the state to discuss common problems, or he attends a state or national meeting where broad educational issues are discussed. Here, he gathers information, gets inspiration, meets old friends, and after it is all over he goes back home feeling that he has a new lease on life.

Meetings dealing with many phases of the educational program are held throughout the year in practically every state. Here, again, there is fragmentation. Interests are specialized. Particular segments of the program are discussed in isolation or out of context with the whole program. One who attends several meetings of this kind over a short period of time will find much duplication, be aware of much lost motion, and, perhaps, be frustrated. These meetings undoubtedly serve a useful purpose. As the bodies of knowledge with which the schools must deal increase in depth, breadth, and intensity, and as specialization increases, the number of such meetings is likely to grow rather than diminish. It is not the intention here to disparage or to reflect disdain on them. Rather, it is the intent to call attention to disintegrating tendencies throughout the educational enterprise and to point out that the true value of these meetings is reflected in what happens to the educational program in the local district back home. The problem is not lack of knowledge of what to do. Rather, it is a problem of how to make the transition from where we are in inservice programs at the present time to where existing knowledge and well-established research strongly indicate inservice programs ought to be.

## Unity in Diversity

The gestalt principle, "the whole is more than the sum of its parts," is no less important in the organization of an inservice program for school administration than in the patterns of psychological behavior in individuals. No individual school in a district can make its fullest contribution toward reaching established educational goals until every staff member contributes to these ends. The kindergarten teacher, the director of guidance, and the head of the department of modern languages have different roles and different tasks to perform. But in the well-administered school, everyone in his own unique way is contributing his best efforts to reaching common goals. The total operation in a school district cannot truly be designated as a system if each school does not serve as an integral part of the system and contribute its full share toward achieving the common district goals.

No state can make continuous progress in its educational endeavor without a broadly planned program based on objectives and goals that give direction to the endeavor and call for the use of all professional resources in the state. W. H. Burnham has expressed a concept that is applicable to such operational policy. Succinctly, he phrases it "a task, a plan, and freedom." An inservice program is not something separate and apart from the regular educational program. In the early planning stages, effort should be made to discover and to develop circumstances in which continued growth of individuals can take place within the context of the total school system. The program that is so conceived and so designed becomes an integral part of what the school system is and what it does.

Someone has aptly said that, if the teacher ceases to be a learner, he ceases to be a teacher. This concept is equally applicable to an administrator. Educational programs are improved by improving people who are responsible for the program. Improvements cannot be accomplished by making changes in the structure alone. A good structure does not in and of itself lead to good schools. At its best, it can do no more than provide a situation in which good schools can be developed. In some instances, structure impedes the development of good educational programs.

Professional growth is most rapid when staff members feel themselves to be a part of an environment in which everyone is attemping to make improvements. Effort to bring about improvement must have direction and objectives. Organization establishes goals and mobilizes the resources for a program, but this is no more than setting the stage. It is the action which follows that counts—action which catches the spirit of staff members, enlists their interests and drives, and gives them the information, insights, or skills they need and want to deal more effectively with the problems that confront them. An inservice program cannot be everything to everybody. It must have unity and a common purpose which every member of the staff accepts as his or her responsibility. It is a growing, dynamic process that is continuously on the move.

The local district is the best setting for an inservice program for school administration for the simple reason that the administrator's overriding responsibility is to provide invigorating leadership within the total school situation. Unless the administrator is willing to proceed on a trial-and-error basis, it becomes necessary, with recurring frequency, that he secure assistance in thinking through and dealing with complicated school problems. Staff members from the institutions of higher education, state departments of education, and professional associations of school administrators should be available to assist him when their help is needed. In some instances, administrators in a number of adjoining districts may find it fruitful to form a council or a study group and cooperatively utilize the services of consultants or join in supporting an inservice program. Whatever the procedure may be, the fundamental point of consideration is how the service affects the people and, in turn, the educational program in the local district. No inservice program is an end in itself. Its central purpose is to provide better educational opportunities for the children in the schools.

The institution of higher education that would cooperate with a local district, a cluster of districts, or groups of school administrators and lend its strength and support in developing an inservice program that is based upon these premises must devise a workable plan of action. The program in Bellevue, Washington, is an illustration of a comprehensive inservice program that was initiated and developed on such premises.

## A Program for a Growing District

The total staff and a great number of lay citizens in Bellevue, Washington, were involved in a comprehensive inservice program, developed and sustained cooperatively by Washington State University and the Bellevue school district. This program blended analysis of existing situations; depth study of the educational needs of the community and careful thinking about the character and quality of a program to meet these needs; and long-range planning that projected into the future the population growth, the location of schools, the procurement of sites, and the school district's problems of financial support. The initial steps in this inservice program were the development of policy, the assignment of responsibilities, and the outlining of general procedures for this total inservice program. For the purposes of clarity, an outline of the basic working agreement showing the relationship between the University and the local school system is included here. The basic purposes were—

1. To provide for the best possible educational opportunities for the youth of the community.

2. To evaluate the present educational program and facilities.

3. To plan a long-range educational program with the counsel and assistance of the community.

4. To keep the community continually informed of problems that are encountered by the school.

When a relatively large number of people participate in group study, it is necessary that responsibility and authority be clearly defined and delegated. Unless this is done, individuals, in their desire to contribute to the betterment of their schools, get in each other's way, duplicate efforts, and forget sources of authority; there is needless confusion and much misunderstanding. When operating relationships are clearly defined, it is much easier to obtain information, to assemble data, to reach conclusions, and to transform conclusions into action.

The operational policy developed and adopted by the school board for the Bellevue inservice program follows.

*Board of Education*

1. The school board is the final authority in all school matters.

2. Policies governing all operation shall be established by the board of education, and all personnel shall operate within these policies until altered by the board.

3. The school board shall not be committed to any policies or proposals that are not acted upon in a regular or special meeting. The board is the final legal authority for operation of the school district.

4. Plans derived from cooperative thinking shall be translated into action.

*Superintendent of Schools*

1. Authority and responsibility for operation of board policies shall be delegated to the superintendent of schools.

2. The superintendent may delegate authority to members of the professional staff, but they are responsible to him.

3. The superintendent shall keep the board well informed on all matters, activities, and developments.

*Consultant-Director* (College or University Staff Member)

1. At all times, the consultant-director works directly with the superintendent of schools or his delegated representative, as directed.

2. He shall appear before the board of education when the superintendent or the board requests his presence.

3. He may recommend procedures and policies only after agreement with the superintendent of schools.

4. All written material that is incorporated in any final report must be submitted to the consultant-director for suggestions.

*Planning Coordinator*

1. The authority and responsibility of the planning coordinator is delegated to him by the superintendent of schools, and he is directly responsible to him.

2. His duties and responsibilities shall be—
   (a) To act as coordinator of the educational planning project.
   (b) To direct the necessary research.
   (c) To organize and act as secretary of all committees.
   (d) To keep a written record and files of all action, recommendations, and plans. (Reports of all committees should be submitted to him.)
   (e) To perform such other duties as the superintendent of schools shall designate and delegate to him.

This inservice program was organized as a long-term study project for the school district. This school system was destined to grow, during the time the study was under way, from a small rural district to a suburban district with an enrollment of 15,000 to 20,000 students. At the time this inservice program was initiated, the administrator and board of education were deeply concerned about planning for this expansion. More than 300 citizens, teachers, and administrators were actively involved in this study and action program that extended over a period of several years and led to—

1. Developing an administrative code for the school district, with job descriptions and staff organization clearly delineated.

2. Developing personnel standards.

3. Defining the responsibilities of school employees.

4. Formulating policies for selection, promotion, and dismissal of personnel.

5. Reshaping and strengthening the guidance program, with provisions made for a well-planned testing program and a follow-up of high school graduates.

6. Improving library services.

7. Developing many curriculum guides.

8. Changing pupil-teacher ratios substantially.

9. Procuring school sites while suitable space was available at reasonable cost.

10. Strengthening and dramatically expanding the adult education program.

11. Giving the citizens of an entire school system faith in the schools, an understanding of school problems and needs, and a belief in the schools that led them to go to the polls 12 successive times and voluntarily increase school taxes to support the educational program they needed and wanted.

This inservice program is a graphic example of planning, doing, and learning on the part of the staff, the board of education, and the citizens of a school district over a period of several years. It is a program that was not organized as specific courses, nor did it provide pat answers. Rather, it was a program that developed as people sought solutions to difficult problems that confronted them in a rapidly growing school district. The University's role, for the most part, was one of stimulation, encouragement, guidance, and assistance wherever and whenever staff members could be helpful. It was a program that helped people face up to the challenges that confronted them and to the responsibilities that were truly theirs.

## Study Councils

In many parts of the country, universities are providing effective services to strengthen and improve school administration through study councils. Study councils usually involve a number of school districts working cooperatively with an institution of higher education. The leadership involved in establishing study councils has, for the most part, come from the universities. This leadership has been simple, direct, and to the point, and, for the most part, has been little more than letting administrators know that assistance is available in the university and can be obtained if and when desired.

In all parts of the country, there are county, regional, and area meetings of superintendents. Often, these are monthly or bimonthly meetings, depending upon the size of the area from which the superintendents come and the availability of transportation. Commonly, staff members from the university attend these meetings. In the discussion during these meetings, attention is called invariably to problems in the local school districts which indicate a need for resources that are available in the university. It may be a survey of research in a special area; it may be compiling reference materials; or it may be getting information on the usefulness and appropriateness of an instructional procedure. Through such channels of communication, university staff members become tuned to field problems and are able to follow through when called upon for assistance. For the purpose of clarification, an example of an area council's actual working relationships is cited here.

## Membership

A school study council will be formed to include all school districts in the area that desire to participate with the university in a cooperative program of educational improvement. This council will be known as the School Study Council. Membership of the Council will be composed of superintendents of participating districts, a representative from the state university, and the county superintendent of schools.

## Purpose of the School Study Council

The purpose of the Study Council will be to assist in providing the best possible education at the local district level by—

1. Providing a structure for cooperative action.
2. Providing consultant service to school board members, administrators, and teachers.
3. Making research data available.
4. Developing high-quality inservice programs for faculties.
5. Experimenting, programming, and evaluating.
6. Bringing to each school district information, services, and personnel not otherwise readily available.

## Criteria for Operation

1. The Study Council will deal with problems of concern to any and all districts, regardless of size.
2. The Council will assist all administrators in relating their programs to the fundamental purposes of American education.
3. The program will assist local districts in looking to the future by compiling and distributing research information and by evaluating existing programs and practices.
4. The program will seek to enlist, involve, and motivate school staffs in the direction of improving education.
5. The Council will provide the machinery, resources, and opportunity to enable local districts to keep pace with new educational programs, equipment, and procedures.

*Some Proposed Activities*

1. Provide school districts with information and research data on educational topics such as ungraded elementary schools, team teaching, use of teaching machines, use of correspondence courses in high school, experiments in teaching, maximum utilization of school facilities, personnel practices, school board policies, education beyond the high school, guidance and counseling techniques, inservice programs for teachers, and evaluation instruments and techniques.

2. Assist local districts in making studies of their own operations, such as adequacy of written policies pertaining to both board and faculty operations, existing inservice programs, methods of attaining fundamental goals, methods of instruction in the various subject-matter fields at all levels, articulation, and the possibilities for the exchange of teachers between two or more school districts.

3. Assist local districts in making use of new equipment and new techniques.

4. Devise sound programs for all students—programs geared to ability of pupils regardless of school size.

5. Provide workshops for administrators and teachers.

6. Determine the number and kinds of resource persons available to each school district, and explore methods of using them in the schools.

*Agencies and Resources Available*

By cooperating with the college of education of the state university, the Council will have access to university personnel, research data, and library material. Graduate students will be encouraged to conduct studies and research in member school systems when requested by the local district. The county superintendent of schools will provide personnel, facilities, and clerical assistance. Local administrators and their faculties comprise a body of professional people with high potential for cooperative action. Experience has shown that personnel from business and industry are available and willing to work with educators when their services are requested.

*Financing the Program*

The basic program, designed to benefit all participating districts, will be financed so that—

1. Dues for each school district will be in the amount of 10 cents per pupil in attendance, with a minimum assessment of $50 and a

maximum of $350 per school district. Money so contributed would be used to cover travel expenses of personnel from the state university on official business with the Study Council.

2. The university will provide a director for the Study Council and assistants and consultants to work with people in the cooperating school systems on educational problems. Transportation will be by university cars at a cost to the Council of 6 cents per mile.

## Other Examples

The Metropolitan School Study Council is an organization of 70 school districts in and around the area of New York City. The Institute of Administrative Research, at Teachers College, Columbia University, under the direction of Dr. Paul Mort, formed this Council.

The Associated Public School Systems of 240 member school districts located throughout the country from coast to coast and the Central School Study Council made up of 375 member school districts in New York State are also centered in the Administrative Research Center at Teachers College.

The New England School Development Council is an organization of school systems in six states that studies educational problems and serves as a clearinghouse for information pertaining to the organization and operation of schools. This Council maintains an executive secretary and has headquarters at Harvard University, Cambridge, Massachusetts.

The Oregon School Study Council, in addition to serving school administrators, gives special attention to the inservice training of school board members. The center is located at the University of Oregon, with a faculty member of the School of Education serving as executive secretary.

The Oregon School Study Council is an agency established cooperatively by sponsoring school districts and the University of Oregon for the purpose of engaging in administrative research as the needs for specific information are revealed by school boards and administrators and requests are made for research undertakings. The Council is in no way an action organization. It confines its activities to the publication of research reports, the distribution to school districts of important recent literature, and the development of conferences in which personnel in the member school systems have a chance to visit among themselves and to discuss various phases of the school program.

The Oregon School Study Council is administered by an executive secretary in accordance with policies established by the governing board. The governing board of the Council is composed of three school superintendents, two school board members of participating school districts elected by the representatives of the member school districts, two members of the staff of the School of Education appointed by the dean, one member of the State Department of Education appointed by the state superintendent of public instruction, and one member of the Oregon School Boards Association appointed by the president.

The operating budget for the Oregon School Study Council during the school year 1961-62 amounted to $16,610. Of this amount, approximately $8,615 was provided by contributions of funds and services from the budget of the School of Education of the University of Oregon. The balance was provided through dues of the participating school districts. Subscription dues for the services of the Council are paid by participating school districts on the basis of 10 cents per child in average daily attendance, with the provision that no school district shall pay less than $50 or more than $250.

## State Associations of School Administrators

To an increasing extent in recent years, institutions of higher education are taking advantage of opportunities to work with state associations of school administrators in the analysis of educational problems and in the development of action programs. This, in part, is an indication of the growing strength of state associations and of their acceptance of a greater measure of responsibility for the total profession of school administration.

The recent amendment to the Constitution of the American Association of School Administrators, which establishes—as a prerequisite to initial active membership after 1964—two years of professional preparation beyond the bachelor's degree, has undoubtedly contributed to this growing concern of state associations. It has called attention to the course content of preservice preparation programs; it has stimulated interest on the part of superintendents now employed to meet this professional requirement; it has called for a review of admission practices and criteria used by school board members for initial employment; and it has led to restudy and revision of standards for the certification of school administrators in many states. Associations of school administrators in almost every state have turned to the colleges and universities to assist them in thinking through these professional problems and in initiating constructive action.

Some graduate students in school administration at universities have accepted invitations to work on specific problems with committees of state associations of school administrators. Some of the problems and projects that have emerged from the deliberations of state associations have led to intensive study and to doctoral theses.

### State School Boards Associations

The National School Boards Association and the respective state school boards associations are newcomers on the educational scene, but they are exercising a very important role in school administration. Institutions of higher education are working closely with these associations. It was Northwestern University that supported the National School Boards Association in its infancy by providing office space and considerable clerical assistance without cost until the organization could get on its feet and under way. In a number of states—particularly in Arkansas, Michigan, New Mexico, Virginia, and West Virginia—a staff member of a college of education has served as executive secretary of the state school boards association. The institutions of higher education and the school boards associations in these states have thus been brought together in close working relationships.

In a more specific illustration of the services of a college of education to a state school boards association, attention is called to the school directors guide in Washington State. The relationship in this particular project was simple and direct. The executive committee of the school boards association, with the advice of the executive secretary and a college of education staff member, appointed a joint handbook committee to develop the guide. The past president of the state school administrators association served as chairman of the committee, and a college staff member served as executive secretary. Other members of the committee included four school directors, a member of the state board of education, a member of the state department of public instruction, and representatives from the secondary school principals association, the elementary school principals association, the teachers association, the county superintendents association, and the school administrators association. A graduate student in school administration at the university used this project for a dissertation topic. Regional meetings held throughout the state to discuss the content of the handbook were a unique feature of this inservice program. Many superintendents attended these meetings. Graduate students, as well as staff members, took part in the discussions. In this manner, the content of the material was revised and rewritten a number of times. The final result was a complete, useful, and highly respected publication entitled *Boardsmanship*.

### Opportunity To Serve

The principles, policies, programs, and projects called to attention and briefly discussed here only suggest possibilities and approaches that institutions of higher education in every state can follow in developing useful inservice programs for school administration. Other examples are pointed out in Chapter 6, and many more could be cited; limitation of space, however, prevents their inclusion.

There is great variation in the character and intensity of inservice programs and wide diversity in the resources used and in the problems that come to the forefront. But wherever one looks, whether it be in the teeming cities, in quiet country towns, or in the wide open spaces of the prairies, there is need for more understanding in every facet of school administration. The problems come with recurring frequency, and each new one seems to be more difficult than those which have preceded it.

If there ever was a time when a college of education could remain nestled quietly among the trees on the campus and serve its rightful role in the culture of a state by waiting for business to come to it, that time has passed. The need for service exists, and the institution of higher education has the resources. To fail to use them in an effective manner when and where they are needed is to fall short of the very purpose for which the institution was created.

# CHAPTER NINE

# The Role of the State
# Department of Education

$I$N a democratic society, power flows from the people. The feelings, the desires, and the values of people are translated through social and political action into instruments that serve them. Organizations, agencies, institutions, and government itself, all creatures of the inventive genius of free-thinking people, are means to ends, not ends in themselves. They have been created to serve people and to maintain conditions under which people can work to best advantage, utilize their energies most effectively, and secure the greatest satisfaction and best results in pursuing their common interests and in meeting their common needs.

School government, one of the most common social instruments in the United States, has been created to bring pupils and teachers together and to mobilize physical resources for educational purposes. The central point of responsibility for public education in every state is the state educational agency. Every state has a chief state school officer and a state department of education. And, in most states, there is a board of education that acts as a policy-forming body. The prime responsibility of the state educational agency is improvement of the schools and the total educational endeavor. It is the agency through which the legislature expresses the will of the people and gives form and order to the state's responsibility for education; it is the agency through which the legislature regulates the schools and through which the state itself operates educational institutions such as those founded primarily for the preparation of teachers for the common schools.

## Dynamics for Growth and Improvement

At almost any given moment in a state, there are many active competing and conflicting interests and many divergent viewpoints. A taxpayers league exerts pressure to keep school taxes as low as possible. A farm organization advocates a sales tax, and labor organizations in the state oppose it. The league of women voters insists on lengthening the school term and giving more emphasis in the curriculum to the humanities. An industrial organization presses for the addition of vocational courses to the high school program, and the state chapter of the American Automobile Association insists that more attention be given to driver training. The parent-teacher association urges that kindergarten classes be added to the instructional program. And the young citizens for democratic action want more attention given to recreational activities. These and a hundred other active interests operating in a state at almost any time are the forces which bring about changes in objectives, changes in function, changes in organization, and changes in curriculum. They are, in effect, the dynamics of school government. Disturbing as they may be at times to those who have responsibility for dealing with them, they constitute the fountainhead of educational growth and improvement.

These forces take tangible form in specific problems that must be faced by school boards and administrators in local districts throughout the state and, in a broad and more general sense, by the state educational agency As the chief state school officer, together with his staff, takes inventory of the problems that press for decision and action at almost any time, he may well find that attention must be given to the education of physically handicapped children, certification of school psychologists, reorganization of local school districts, state aid for the construction of school buildings, a change in the formula for the apportionment of state school moneys, the establishment of regional vocational schools, financial support for a junior college, adult education, procurement of school buses, a change in the teacher-retirement program, improving the supervisory services in rural schools, strengthening the program of foreign language instruction in the secondary schools, activating the provisions in the Manpower Development and Training Act, tuition for summer school attendance, and a 12-month school term.

These and a host of other problems confront school board members and administrators in local school districts throughout the state. They call for factual information, further insight, deeper understanding, and decision and action that are in conformity with school laws, broad educational policy, and the best interests of people in each and every local district and in the state as a whole. Through jointly seeking solutions, a large measure of inservice growth takes place on the part of school administrators and everybody else concerned with the schools.

## Leadership

This is not the place to outline the authority and functions of the state educational agency in detail. It is sufficient to point out that the functions of the state educational agency are, in general, regulation, research and data gathering, administration of special services, and leadership. The vitality and, indeed, the very life of the state educational agency lies in its leadership function. In emphasizing the importance of this function in a state educational enterprise, Thurston and Roe have said:

With the philosophy of creative leadership instilled in all members, the state office can fan into life within the state a growing, dynamic, and inspired educational force. Without it the deadening pall of bureaucracy, regulation, red tape and restrictions can stifle creativity. Leadership can mobilize, unify, and coordinate all the positive forces concerned with education for the dedicated purpose of its improvement. It can give common direction to the efforts of all. It can analyze the nature and future direction of education and communicate with the public in this regard. It can foster local initiative by discovering and publicizing improved practices and encourage others to follow suit. It can utilize all possible resources for experimentation and improvement. It can provide opportunities and stimulate all persons engaged in educational work to grow and create professionally.[1]

The National Council of Chief State School Officers, in analyzing the leadership function of state departments of education, calls attention to the importance of planning, research, consultation and advice, coordination, public relations, and inservice education.[2] As essential facts are gathered and analyzed, as immediate and long-range plans are projected, as the efforts of various groups and institutions are coordinated, and as ways are devised for increasing public understanding of the educational enterprise, people are involved, understanding is increased, and professional growth takes place.

The state educational agency is responsible to all of the people of the state; it serves everybody; and, if it performs its leadership function well, the basis for decision and action is strengthened and improved. This broad, state-wide leadership responsibility can never be pushed into the background or treated lightly. With this in mind, the discussion here, nevertheless, will be restricted to the part the state educational agency can play in the improvement of school administration. But once again, it should be emphasized that everything the state educational agency does that involves individuals, groups of people, local educational author-

[1] Thurston, Lee M., and Roe, William E. *State School Administration.* New York: Harper & Brothers, 1957. p. 82.
[2] National Council of Chief State School Officers. *The State Department of Education.* Washington, D.C.: the Council, 1952. p. 21.

ities, and the general public is, in effect, directed toward the improvement of administration and the operation of the schools.

It is not only unnecessary but unwise to consider the leadership function of the state department of education as distinct from its regulatory function. Time and time again, it is through exercise of its regulatory function that the state carries on its most effective program for the improvement of school administration. To illustrate, the state agency is charged with responsibility for the certification of teachers, for the approval or accreditation of schools and colleges, for assuring a minimum program both in quality and scope and ascertaining that procedures required in this accomplishment are followed, for requiring the hiring of personnel with proper qualifications, for insuring that standards for the health and safety of children and teachers be maintained in the construction and operation of school buildings, for enforcing the compulsory attendance laws, for safeguarding the public's investment in the educational enterprise through proper accounting of school funds, and for seeing that the basic legal requirements for the operation of schools are met. All states have responsibilities of this kind that must be met.

The performance of such functions may well suggest inspection, checking up on people, management, and control. And, indeed, in years past, the exercise of regulatory functions by some state departments of education had some of these characteristics. But as leadership has been strengthened and people have been helped to see and understand the fundamental reasons for these precautionary measures, this aspect of control has taken on a new meaning. It has released the energies of people, caused them to be imaginative and creative, and brought new resources to the schools, with the result that minimum standards again and again have been surpassed, and the total educational program has moved ahead to higher levels of effectiveness and quality.

State agencies must establish regulations for new programs mandated by their respective legislatures, such as programs for the retarded and the gifted; for educational television; and for teaching the English language, American history, and citizenship. But here again, there is rich opportunity for strengthening the principles and improving the processes of school administration through collective action. It is of the utmost importance, rather than spell out procedures in detail, that the legislation be so drawn that it authorizes the state agency to set up regulations through which school administration can function. Furthermore, it is important that all educational interests in the state support the agency in securing such legislation. Legislation which prescribes the content of the curriculum and provides for the details of administration is inflexible and unwise. Programs governed in detail by statute rather than by regulation are hard to change. They become outmoded, more expensive to operate than need be, and, in general, they miss the mark at which they are aimed.

## Working with People

The state educational agency must devise ways and means for working with people. It must draw upon the information and leadership potential that reside in the people of the state.  It must enlist the support and draw upon the strength of as many people as possible. This is, indeed, the prime function of leadership.  Many state agencies have found it not only advisable but exceptionally useful to set up advisory councils or committees to assist in drawing up regulations, to aid in administering these regulations, and to recommend modifications as the need arises. For example, there are in many states certification advisory councils or committees representing the profession and the public.  Representatives on such councils come from such state organizations as the superintendents association, elementary and secondary principals associations, the teachers association, and the school boards association.

Problems with far-reaching implications that come before the certification advisory council may originate with some special group of people in the state. To illustrate, the foreign language teachers, in their zeal to improve instruction, may suggest upgrading requirements for their own certification.  Such proposals should be referred to the council and carefully studied for their merits as well as for the problems that might be created by suggested changes. The council, together with the state educational agency, in reviewing these recommendations, must forthrightly face such questions as whether or not changes in certification standards would improve instruction, whether or not they would bring about conditions that would make it impossible to staff the schools, and whether or not they would adversely affect the total curriculum offerings.

## State-Wide Committees

In some states, committees have been established by state educational agencies to draw up standards for the educational specifications of school buildings. In developing these standards, the committee carefully reviews and thinks through the provisions that should be made for sanitation, fire safety, heating and ventilation, and learning space most appropriate for instruction. The work of such a committee may lead to revision of the building code or to developing a guide for construction. Such committees may well include representatives from the building industry, the architects association, organized labor, and governmental officials who work along with the school administrators and school plant specialists in thinking through school plant problems. The state agency that takes the initiative in getting such committee work under way and making the findings and recommendations known often precludes the legislature's stepping into the void and mandating independent state commissions that vie with each other and the state board in developing such standards.

In directing attention to the total educational program through such probing questions, greater understanding of the factors involved in maintaining appropriate balance in the educational program of the state is developed. It is upon the basis of such analysis of a problem that the chief state school officer finally makes his recommendations to the state board of education. Final authority rests with the state and cannot be abdicated to an advisory council. The over-all responsibility for the general public interest must be exercised by the state authority. There can be no thought of the state's turning over its responsibilities to professional associations or to any other organizations. Nevertheless, much of the talent for improvement resides in professional associations, and its use should be encouraged as well as its potential for growth actively fostered and cultivated. The state educational agency operates most effectively when it draws freely upon the best and most widely representative thinking available in reaching its decisions. In such fashion, the educational interests of the state are served best, and all persons who have assisted the state department have profited.

### Accreditation

Another example of an activity with rich potential for professional growth in states where resources are great enough to permit the function to be performed well is the evaluation of schools and colleges for accreditation or approval by the state. After the school, school system, or institution of higher learning has completed the procedures of self-evaluation, using an approved set of standards such as state standards for secondary schools or the standards of the National Cooperative Study of Secondary Schools, a visiting committee with rotating membership should be formed to meet with representatives of the unit or system being evaluated. This is an extremely worthwhile experience. It has educational value for personnel in the institution and for the evaluators as well. It leads to improvement, not only of those being evaluated, but also of the evaluators. Cooperative evaluation is an excellent device for providing concrete experience that may lead to the spread of improved practice.

Although the regional accrediting associations have been able to improve quality where states could not or would not do so, opportunities for professional growth that accrue to the evaluators have become more restricted. In other words, the desire for speedy approval and the load carried by the large accrediting agency have cut back the benefits that come to the people involved. But even where responsibility for accreditation rests largely with strong regional associations, many of the valuable effects can be secured by greater participation of state department officials. The state department can and should take the lead in doing much of the spadework.

Admitting the advantages—and there are many—of regional and national accreditation, they do fall short in developing the spirit of cooperation and the depth of understanding that can be acquired when the state accepts a larger measure of responsibility for this function. No matter where responsibility for accreditation is placed, the state can and should play an important role in helping the people who are responsible for the schools and colleges overcome apathy and confusion and in clarifying the principles and issues that have been involved in accreditation. Functioning in this manner, the state educational agency can stimulate and strengthen the values of local initiative and local pride and project the limitations and shortcomings in a school district or an institution that has been identified in the accreditation process as stimulating challenges rather than disheartening disappointments.

Clearly, the state must exercise its regulatory functions, but leadership rather than the exercise of authority should color the performance at every point. Exercise of the regulatory function by a state department of education by no means implies wresting control away from the people in the local school district. To the contrary, its purpose is to maintain balance among the many interest groups in society, to relieve tensions, to release creative energies, to coordinate efforts, to see that the rights of every individual are safeguarded, and to insure that the interest of the people in every segment of the state is fairly and adequately represented in educational policy.

Truly, the state has the authority *de jure* to secure compliance. *De facto*, however, this may not work out. It may not be able to establish a large enough organization to do so; if it does, and exerts all of its power, this may become burdensome and aggravating to the local units of government and lead to steps by these units through which the legislature reduces the authority of the state agency. By concentrating on leadership and sustaining large-scale programs through which members of the profession and responsible representatives of the public participate in the formulation of policies and development of procedures that actually take effect, the agency really performs its regulatory function better than it could otherwise, while conducting, at the same time, an efficient program of upgrading school administration.

### Strengthening the Profession

Historically, inservice education for school personnel has been an important state function. Early in his career as a chief state school administrator, Henry Barnard, who established the educational agencies in Connecticut and Rhode Island, initiated teacher institutes. These institutes were designed to give some professional preparation to teachers who had none at all. He supplemented this inservice program by initiating the publication of state educational journals. Later, in Wisconsin, he was instrumental in beginning the development of a national organization of teachers and the first national educational journal.

The normal school, first envisioned by Horace Mann in Massachusetts and later developed in other states, was a direct move by the state educational agency to strengthen and improve instruction in the elementary schools. In the beginning, these institutions served both a preservice and an inservice function. While a large part of the student body consisted of people who were preparing for an initial teaching assignment, many experienced teachers enrolled in the summer programs of the normal schools to better their own professional preparation. It was here that demonstration of superior teaching could be observed.

### Assisting Professional Groups

Although professional associations are participating, to an increasing degree, in conferences and workshops of an inservice nature that are designed to improve instruction, state agencies are still relied upon for stimulation, organization, and leadership in planning these activities. Members of the state departments of education should be assigned as consultants to work with such independent state association groups as science teachers, foreign language teachers, teachers of social studies, elementary school principals, secondary school principals, guidance officers, and mathematics teachers. Frequently, these staff members make their most effective contribution toward improving instruction in the state by working in this capacity with these specialized groups. Such inservice programs are not particularly or immediately dramatic in nature, but they are extremely effective in the long run.

It is not only the various teacher organizations that are served in this manner; the organizations of superintendents, principals, school board members, state citizens advisory councils, and parent groups have also been supported and strengthened.

Several years ago in Connecticut, the practice of assigning a member of the State Department of Education to work on a part-time basis with the state association of school administrators was begun. This staff member's work with the association was under the direction and control of the executive committee of the state association.

This direct assistance in making the association of school administrators more effective in dealing with the problems of vital concern to them has proven over the years to be one of the most useful leadership measures instituted in the state for strengthening and improving school administration and bringing about better solutions to important educational problems. In this manner, the state association of school administrators is helped to find the focus it is looking for. Their efforts are coordinated into a unified movement toward the advancement of the entire educational enterprise. Pluralism—the existence of different points of view and different emphases—brings strengths rather than weaknesses as long as a means is found of keeping administration focused on broad common goals. This is a part of the leadership function.

*State-Wide Conferences*

Last year, the superintendents in the state of Maine met together in their fiftieth annual conference. A half century ago, Payson Smith, who was then chief state school officer, initiated this annual conference. Travel expenses, the cost of lodging, and honorariums for consultants, since the very beginning, have been borne completely by the state educational agency. At the early conferences, the problems discussed may largely have been devoted to such simple matters as methods of gathering information, making reports to the state department, handling school finance, and establishing procedures for purchasing and procuring the equipment used in the schools. There is no apology to be made for this type of program. These were problems at that time, and helping superintendents to think them through clearly so that practices would be improved was a useful and highly important inservice program. Over the years, as the professional preparation of superintendents has risen to higher levels, the nature of the problems discussed in these annual conferences has changed. But they still serve the same function of improving school administration and strengthening the leadership of individual administrators that was in the mind of this great chief state school officer at the time the program was initiated.

Numerous examples of such state conferences could be cited. The mountaintop conference in the state of Washington that was instituted by Pearl Wanamaker when she served as chief state school officer in this state has almost become an institution. It can almost be said that there is no state in which the superintendents do not come together at one or more times during the year to think through important educational problems with the chief state school officer and his staff. In some states, regional groups of administrators are formed, and staff members of state departments of education work with them on more specific educational problems.

### Orientation Program

Every year, there are new superintendents—new to the state or new to their positions. State departments of education, with growing frequency, plan orientation meetings for these superintendents. At the meetings, newcomers have opportunity to meet their peers, to become acquainted with state department personnel, and to get first-hand acquaintance with some of the major problems and issues before the state.

The program for such an orientation meeting may well consist of more or less formal presentations made by personnel in charge of general and special grants, certification, school buildings, curriculum services, pupil personnel services, and research. Through these presentations, the new superintendents become familiarized with the forms that are commonly used in transmitting information to the state and the procedures whereby information is transmitted by the state department to the local districts. Usually, these orientation meetings operate in a climate of easy friendliness. There may be a social hour, a luncheon, or a dinner meeting. Superintendents hear and meet representatives of the state teachers association, of the school boards association, and representatives of other associations in the state. The end result is that they rapidly get an understanding of the manner and methods through which the school administrators work together on educational problems and of how superintendents can be mutually helpful. Only the state agency can successfully set the stage for such an orientation meeting.

Quite early in their period of service, new superintendents are invited to become active members of the superintendents association, are urged to attend zone meetings of superintendents, and are given an opportunity to participate in workshops and the annual meetings of the superintendents association. In a number of states, area and state programs for school administrators are developed with the help of representatives from the state departments of education and consultants from the universities.

*Pooling Efforts*

These inservice activities are not restricted to school administrators. In Wisconsin, for example, the State Department of Education holds an institute for school board members in each county of the state. In other instances, the state department may unite with the university in jointly sponsoring and supporting workshops, institutes, and conferences for school board members and administrators. Such approaches have been common in states where active programs of school district reorganization have been under way. It was through such conferences that standards and criteria for newly formed districts and the step-by-step procedures involved in bringing about the unification of several similar districts into a larger administrative unit have been cooperatively developed and established as working principles.

In recent years, state departments of education in every part of the country have joined with professional associations of school administrators and, in particular, with the American Association of School Administrators in establishing broad approaches to improving the profession of school administration. With eligibility for membership in AASA set by a constitutional amendment at two years of work beyond the baccalaureate degree in an accredited institution, many state departments promptly moved to revise certification requirements. In a bulletin dated August 10, 1962, the Committee for the Advancement of School Administration reported that 20 states required academic preparation beyond the master's degree for the certification of school superintendents and that state commissioners of education in 17 other states indicated that serious consideration was being given to revision of certification standards.[3]

State commissioners of education in the New England states have been active in developing the New England cooperative program for the preservice preparation of school administrators, in which colleges and uni-

---

[3] Committee for the Advancement of School Administration. *Journey That Must Not End.* Washington, D.C.: American Association of School Administrators, a department of the National Education Association, August 10, 1962. (Mimeo.) 10 pp.

versities throughout the region will work together under common policy toward this broad purpose.

And it should be pointed out here that the Council of Chief State School Officers has officially joined AASA and the NEA Department of Rural Education in sponsoring the series of drive-in conferences for community school administrators that has successfully operated over a period of about 15 years.

### Consultative Services

Providing technical information and professional counsel for administrators, school board members, and lay citizens through consultative services is one of the more important functions of the state department of education. In most state departments, there are people who are specialists in such fields as school buildings, transportation, vocational education, elementary education, secondary education, and, in states where such programs are active, school district reorganization. In large state departments, there are many more fields of specialization than in the smaller state departments. Through providing information and assistance, educational leadership is exerted which, in almost every instance, has some of the attributes of an inservice program.

Consultative services have the effect of stimulating action, lessening the chances for costly errors, and assisting people in finding solutions to their own problems. Consultative services help people help themselves rather than attempt to do the job for them. They provide essential information and helpful advice to people who still retain the power of decision and who have final responsibility for the course of action to be followed. In many respects, the provision of consultative services is not unlike the services of a pilot in directing a large ocean liner into dock in the harbor. The pilot guides the vessel through the narrow opening, but, if the vessel runs aground, the captain of the ship is still responsible.[4]

Consultative services, for the purposes of discussion here, may be divided into two general categories: administrative services and instructional services.

### Administrative Services

Administrative services in most state departments of education include research and statistics; assistance with school building planning; inter-

---

[4] Cooper, Shirley, and Fitzwater, C. O. *County School Administration*. New York: Harper & Brothers, 1954. p. 223.

pretation of school law; certification; advice on local administrative organization and practice; working relationships between school boards, administrators, and teachers; and assistance with disputes and controversies of all kinds. Most educational problems that demand the attention of state agencies and that are not clearly of an instructional nature can be classified as problems that draw upon administrative services.

In the provision of consultative services, the state department of education can frequently work to good advantage through representative organizations and through advisory committees. It is not uncommon for consultants from the state department of education to have special assignments to work with the state association of school administrators, the state school boards association, and the state congress of parents and teachers. Staff members with such assignments meet regularly with the executive committees of these associations. It should be pointed out, however, that services are not imposed upon these organizations. Consultants stand ready to serve them upon request. In this way, the state department of education maintains close working relationships with these organizations, supplies them with information when needed, and is able to unite the efforts of different groups with common interests in support of projects.

As one illustration of the many that could be cited, the state department, through such working relationships, may assist in the orientation of new school board members to their duties and responsibilities. It is true that this function can be and is carried on by local boards together with their superintendents, but these local efforts become more effective when supplemented by regional meetings planned with the assistance of the state agency and supported by its prestige. Through such consultative services, the state agency can be helpful to the local district without any threat to its autonomy or independence.

*Policies commission.* The relationship between the state association of school administrators and the state department of education has been mentioned earlier. This relationship is so vital to the total function of school administration in the state that it does not seem out of place to emphasize it further here. Since school superintendents serve at the focal points of school administration in every section of the state, it is desirable to have a state educational policies commission made up of leaders designated by superintendents themselves and by the chief state school officer. The chief state school officer and the president of the state association of school administrators should be members of this policies commission. The commission should meet regularly, possibly four or five times during the school year, and should be continuously concerned with the development of policies to be adopted by the superintendents association and to be recommended for adoption by the state board of education and local school boards.

Experience with policies commissions such as those described shows that attention is directed primarily to problems and questions affecting the entire state—for example, teaching of controversial issues, use of educational television, experimentation with programed instruction, and team teaching. The rationale behind establishing and sustaining a policies commission is that superintendents, by the very nature of their positions, are expected to exercise professional leadership not only with their respective staffs but also in working with their school boards and communities. It is through such a unified approach that the talents of the profession and the research facilities of the state can be combined to carry on a program of inquiry, a program of fact finding, and a program of development that could not be well sustained or operated in any other manner. Committees of principals, teachers, and consultants from local school systems, as well as specialists from the state department of education, work on the development of policies under and through the leadership of such a commission. Through probing and penetrating into the recesses of difficult and perplexing problems and through striving for broader vision and greater perspective, realistic problems and sometimes possible solutions are called to the attention of graduate departments of education in the universities. The state as a whole profits from the commission's work, and professional growth on the part of everybody involved takes place at every point.

*Special committees.* Quite commonly, state departments of education establish special committees comprised of governmental officials, representatives of the building industry, the state architects association, representatives from organized labor, and the teaching profession to think through school building problems. Through such committee work, school building codes have been revised and brought more nearly up to date, educational specifications have been improved, and the standards for school construction have been brought more nearly into line with the actual needs of the educational program. Through coming to grips with these realistic problems and working through them to final solutions, better understanding of the factors involved is developed, and the professional abilities of people have been enhanced.

*Publications.* From time to time in every state, information must be brought together, thinking must be organized, and points of view, expressed in pamphlets, monographs, and bulletins on educational problems. As an illustration, there may be a handbook on working relationships between superintendents and school board members, curriculum guides, and manuals on some phase of financial accounting or personnel management. The staff members of the state department of education might well prepare such publications themselves, but, in so doing, rich opportunities for the professional growth of members of an *ad hoc* committee would be lost; and, at the same time, they would seriously risk having a poor publication. Functions such as these are better performed through cooperative ventures led by the state agency than through direct action by state department personnel.

## Instructional Services

Teachers and administrators in the local school districts perhaps constitute the most valuable source of instructional leadership in the state. Through their daily contacts with pupils in the classroom in actual teaching-learning situations and their familiarity with curriculum content, they are sensitive to the accomplishments of the schools as well as to educational needs that go unmet in every part of the state. With professional preparation programs rapidly improving year after year, they are well acquainted with the principles of learning and with educational theory and have much knowledge of the educational research that exists in their respective fields.

In providing instructional services to professional people such as they, the great challenge to state department personnel is in finding ways and means of utilizing this rich experience, of broadening perspectives, of seeing specific problems in broad context, and of pointing up the relationship between activities in one classroom or in a local school system and the educational endeavor of the state as a whole. Thus, instructional services truly become leadership services.

This leadership may function through committees as attacks are made upon specific problems. It may involve long-range planning, such as developing guides for instructional programs in speech, hearing, school social work, and guidance. It concentrates the full professional strength that resides in people and, in using this strength, adds new dimensions to it at the same time. It focuses attention on a problem to be solved or a goal to be reached rather than on the strengths or deficiencies of individual personalities; and it makes professional growth a joint experience of teachers and administrators.

## The Legislature

The first responsibility of the state educational agency to the legislative assembly is to serve as an instrument for research and development in educational matters. As the state agency carries on the study and research necessary to develop legislative programs, however, it seldom operates alone. Good state agencies have legislative councils comprised of representatives from such organizations and interest groups as the state association of school boards; the state association of superintendents, principals, and teachers; the state congress of parents and teachers; taxpayers organizations; and other groups of lay citizens who have a vital concern about public education.

The authorized representatives from these groups bring to the council the interests, concerns, and proposals for legislative action of the bodies they represent. Proposals are checked against each other and, through discussion and deliberation, a coordinated legislative program is hammered out. Although there may be some disagreement in the end, there is more understanding than would otherwise be possible; and coordinated support of legislative proposals developed in this manner is more likely. In circumstances where it is necessary, coordinated opposition to legislative proposals that are generally regarded as unwise or disadvantageous to the educational program is more easily developed and better understood. Representatives of organizations who participate in this kind of cooperative action profit through a broader and more general view of the nature and needs of public education. A depth and breadth of understanding greater than could otherwise be acquired is achieved. Through rotation on councils and committees from year to year, many people are afforded the benefits of these experiences.

Such legislative councils cannot work to good advantage, alone and unaided. If the full potential that resides in the men and women who devote their time to state-wide educational planning and the factual information that they have at hand are used to best advantage, the state department must supply competent personnel to do the essential staff work for the council. Such experience is educational not only for the people from the organizations involved but for the members of the legislature who have brought before them information and well-formed opinion from many parts of the state. The legislature may modify the educational program that is proposed or may reject a major part or all of it, but decisions will be made on the basis of better and more accurate information than would have been possible without the advice of the council.

## The Public

Although there are many conferences, institutes, workshops, and study groups designed to secure active participation of the public in the initial stages of educational planning, none can substitute for conferences held by the state educational agency. In Connecticut, these conferences are open to the public, and special invitations are extended to leaders from industry, business, government, labor, and political organizations, as well as to educational leaders. Conference programs are developed around problems and issues with state-wide interest, such as financial support of education, improvement of instruction, evaluation of the schools, and new horizons in the curriculum. Their purposes are to gather information, to become sensitive to the currents of educational interests in various segments of the population, to clarify goals, and to move a little closer to common agreement on programs of action.

The conference usually begins with a keynote address in which major problems and issues before the state are called to attention and set in perspective, but the heart of the conference program is the give-and-take discussion in the small sectional meetings. The conference ends with a series of recommendations which reflect the viewpoint and the consensus of the people who have been involved. Newspaper reports from the conference and the conference proceedings, which are published and widely distributed stimulate, through a kind of chain reaction, discussion of educational problems in neighborhoods and communities throughout the state.

The discussions in such state-wide conferences tend to be more objective and attendance more comprehensive than in conferences sponsored by groups with specialized interests or by groups representing a particular geographic area. In a sense, they constitute a broadly oriented inservice program for everyone who is directly or indirectly involved and are a vital link in the whole process of state educational leadership.

## That Extra 5 Percent

Even a casual review of the leadership activities of state departments of education clearly shows that a multitude of activities are carried on year after year which, in one way or another, add to the professional competencies of school administrators and strengthen the whole process of school administration. This, indeed, is a major purpose of the state department of education, for it is through this whole complex process of planning, organizing, operating, managing, and evaluating the educational program that school administration functions. And as this function is improved at any point or in any facet of the operation, the broad educational goals of the state are more nearly approached. But to conclude from such observations that state departments of education are doing everything that ought to be done to add to the professional growth of school administrators would be shortsighted and misleading, and a grossly inadequate reflection of the leadership potential of the state educational agency.

The very pressure of events focuses attention more often than not on the here and now—on the problems calling for immediate attention. This is as it ought to be. Unless the problems immediately at hand are attended to and dealt with in proper manner, there can be no sound foundation on which to stand to reach for higher goals. The limitations in the inservice programs now under way in most states reflect the pressures of the moment. However, in an increasing number of instances, men and women are relieved of and freed from their jobs for short periods of time to meet together to think through—with free and untrammeled minds—broad and comprehensive social problems and issues. The intent of such inservice activities is to stretch the imaginations of people, to build in new dimensions of power, and to reach out toward what lies beyond.

Business and industrial leaders concerned about the vitality of their enterprises frequently speak of that extra 5 percent. Whether they are referring to the competencies of personnel or the total complex of organization and operation, that extra 5 percent tends to be an element of a qualitative nature. It is that element which is above and beyond the minimum requirements of day-to-day operations, the plus factor that reflects a glow of vitality and has within it the potential for moving forward toward higher achievement. It is a blend of confidence, efficiency, spirit, and imagination moved forward with high purpose.

Perhaps it is that extra 5 percent that state departments of education are seeking as they look anew at their programs of inservice education for school administration. Toynbee has suggested that it is the administrator who can rise above his daily task and see his institution with a fresh eye who is capable of providing the energy and drive to keep it moving forward. Unfortunately, many school superintendents are so harassed with immediate problems and issues that they do not have the time or energy needed for getting fresh insights and new inspirations and for cultivating vitality.

It is at this point that serious attention is needed as programs of inservice education are reshaped. The ability to recognize genuine needs and realistic problems as challenges and as opportunities for constructive and forward-moving action is an attribute of successful leadership at every level of school administration and, in particular, at the state level. To initiate and sustain a program of activities and experiences through which the school administrators of a state can gain new perspectives of their jobs and the strength to tackle them with fresh vigor is a central purpose of the state department of education's inservice program. Such programs will be developed only through creative thinking and imaginative planning. In developing them, state superintendents of public instruction will turn to superintendents and other educational leaders in the state for assistance, just as they have turned to them again and again for help in meeting other educational challenges.

As programs of inservice education for school administration are more thoroughly explored, it is easy to envision in the years immediately ahead wider adoption of policies through which administrators are given leaves of absence to engage in study, in planning, and in seminars in which the educational implications of broad cultural problems are explored. The intent will be to add to the reservoir of educational leadership upon which school boards, instructional staff members, and communities of people are incessantly drawing for inspiration, counsel, and guidance in educational matters.

CHAPTER

TEN

# The Role of the
# Professional Organization

**A** PROFESSIONAL organization of school administrators is, in effect, a voluntary association of people who have primary responsibility for educational leadership, particularly leadership of an executive nature. These men and women have joined together in common effort for common purposes. The only real justification for any individual's joining with a state or the national association of school administrators is to accomplish purposes that he cannot achieve by working alone. An association is strongest and most effective when its membership is actively involved in doing something about problems or issues that really count.

In every state, there are one or more state-wide associations of school administrators, and, in many states, there are regional groups of administrators that meet together at regular intervals and carry forward programs of professional activities from year to year. While there is no structural or formal relationship between regional and state associations and the American Association of School Administrators, all these diverse groups have developed a sense of unity through effort to reach common goals.

Professional leadership looms large among the functions of the American Association of School Administrators. By its constitution, the Association is committed to—

1. Elevating the professional and ethical standards of the teaching profession in general and administrative and supervisory services in particular.

2. Achieving unity in professional strength for the improvement of education.

3. Developing and maintaining understanding of the vital relationship of the culture in general to education.

4. Placing before the public facts and viewpoints that will lead to thorough understanding of the schools and intelligent action on educational problems.

160

5. Strengthening the institution of public education and improving the schools.

The growing acceptance for a larger measure of responsibility by state associations for the qualifications, competencies, and professional conduct of school administrators and for the status and prestige of the total profession has been one of the most remarkable and encouraging developments on the educational scene in recent years. No longer are state associations content merely to act as pressure groups, exhausting their energies in bringing about adjustments in formulas for distributing state school moneys, or to commit their full resources to bringing about changes in administrative organization. While these are important concerns to organizations of administrators, and forever must be, these groups, to a growing extent, are showing greater interest in developing and sustaining the standards of a true profession.

Leo E. Buehring, writing in the September 1962 issue of *The Nation's Schools*, reports that associations of school administrators in 42 of the 50 states either have taken steps to make two years of graduate study a condition of membership in their associations or had the matter under active discussion at the time of writing.[1] Each state has an active committee on standards of professional preparation. These committees, working through their respective state associations, are actively engaged in—

1. Developing and getting acceptances of codes of ethics for the profession.
2. Bringing about improvements in certification standards.
3. Strengthening and improving the preservice preparation programs for school administrators.
4. Developing and sustaining internship programs.
5. Formulating criteria that may be used by local school boards to good advantage in the employment of school administrators.
6. Developing inservice education programs.

It is to these voluntary associations of professional people that this discussion is particularly addressed.

*Roads To Improvement*

Improvement in school administration can best be made after the extent and nature of present deficiencies are ascertained and assessed. There is

---

[1] Buehring, Leo E. "Some Giant Steps Are Being Taken Toward Making School Administration a Real Profession." *Nation's Schools:* 70: 112; September 1962.

much useful information available for help in determining this basic point of departure for developing inservice programs for school administration. During the last decade, numerous studies have been made under the auspices of foundations and universities. A survey of the findings of these investigations reveals several inadequacies in contemporary school administration.

*Knowledge.* Some administrators are lacking in broad knowledge not only in educational administration and supervision but also in the arts, sciences, and humanities. There is also evidence in some administrators of an inability to draw upon knowledge from disciplines other than the discipline of professional education. Concurrent with these limitations is a tendency to disregard, or at least to fail to utilize, the findings of pertinent research. The administrator, often beset by a continuous stream of operational problems, rationalizes inability to strive for outstanding competence in at least one area of specialization. This failure to be especially competent in some field of knowledge tends to downgrade him as a leader.

*Performance skills.* The behavioral sciences have provided much useful information about the way people feel and act in the performance of their duties. Administrators do not turn to these sources frequently enough and are themselves often lacking in some of the behavioral skills of leadership.

*Judgment.* The school administrator is continuously called upon to make difficult decisions, often under considerable pressure. Good judgment is a critical factor in administrative decision making. Ill-timed decisions are costly; failure to anticipate problems and issues is often crucial; and the inability to evaluate community forces properly is a hazard of considerable proportion.

*Administrative effectiveness.* High-level administrative efficiency requires the delegation of responsibility. Lack of courage and self-confidence that leads administrators to keep too many details of administration in their own hands and to fail to delegate responsibilities appropriately is detrimental to administrative effectiveness and generates deficiencies in the art of problem solving.

*Conceptions.* Among all the inadequacies in school administration that could be mentioned, none is more serious than the failure of the superintendent to continue to gain knowledge and understanding of the broad problems of education.

No good purpose can be served here in trying to catalogue or classify the weaknesses in administration that have been revealed by research or that can be noted by keen observers. Those identified above suffice to illustrate the need to strive for correction, correction particularly of these deficiencies which are the most significant.

## Meeting Needs

It is easier to identify deficiencies and the need for improvement in administrative operation than it is to see, to understand, and to remove shortcomings in the personal qualities of executives that are so vital to the character and quality of the whole process of administration. Administrators commonly seek to correct their inadequacies and to improve their professional capabilities by taking specific university courses, by attending workshops designed for concentrated emphasis upon certain problems, or by trying to get more information on topics being discussed in conferences and conventions. Such efforts are fine as far as they go, but they are not enough.

A successful program of inservice growth for administrators, as conceived in the context of this chapter, goes deeper and is more subtle. Knowing the difference between a more-or-less obvious "surface" leadership inadequacy and one that is a basic underlying cause of deficiency is of crucial importance. As the problem is pondered, it is tempting to conclude that the reason for overemphasizing the more obvious and underestimating the subtler causes of administrative inadequacy is a result of misconceiving the proper role of the educational leader. Perhaps administrators tend to view their roles with too narrow a perspective and fail to see them in their broader and larger dimensions—fail to see the school superintendent in a peer relationship with other leaders in the community's social, business, and political life. Improvement of the school administrator is more likely to come when he views his role in the larger spectrum of both the community and society in general.

### A Program of Services

The suggestion made above that inservice growth activities for school administrators embrace more than what is currently being done is not meant to depreciate existing efforts. Rather, it is a proposal to supplement what is now going on under the auspices of universities, state departments of education, and the many fine professional organizations in this country. The extent of these efforts is a manifestation of the enthusiasm of many dedicated professional people working to strengthen educational leadership in this country.

The school administrator himself must feel and accept a personal responsibility for his own professional growth and development. He, of course, cannot do this unaided and alone; he must work with like-minded colleagues, impelled and motivated by a strong inner urge to raise the level of educational leadership in this country.

Just as with preservice programs for school administrators and the preparation programs for the other professions, some portion of the expense of an inservice program for school administration should undoubtedly be borne by state departments of education, tax-supported colleges and universities, and local school districts. Such expenditures are investments that society makes in the people upon whom it depends for professional services and high-quality leadership. This is a fundamental reason for establishment of colleges and universities at public expense. The value of these contributions cannot be overestimated, but, above and beyond these efforts, additional efforts must be made by national and state associations of school administrators. It is from these professional groups that much of the initiative must come for developing and sustaining the inservice programs herein proposed.

The national and state associations of school administrators have unique opportunity to be in the vanguard of efforts to raise the qualitative levels of educational leadership. All members of these associations have opportunity and should feel a commitment to—

1.  Work cooperatively for the improvement of educational programs for *all* children.

2.  Understand more clearly the dynamics and dimensions of educational leadership.

3.  Be involved in a comprehensive program of professional growth activities that stress not only increased professional knowledge but also the improvement of the skills of leadership performance.

4.  Develop school administration as a profession to a point wherein it is regarded and respected on a full-peer level with executive leadership in other professions.

5.  Share in the development of a code of ethical behavior to which all may subscribe, and demonstrate by their performance a high regard for the profession of educational administration.

Assuming these purposes worthy and possible of attainment, it follows that concerted efforts should be made to achieve them. A good beginning has already been made. The standards which have been established for admission into the profession of educational administration—the AASA membership requirement, in particular—serve as a foundation for further improvement of the profession.

It must not be assumed, however, that high admission standards are enough. Membership must carry with it a commitment on the part of each administrator to work for continued personal improvement. If the profession is to grow and develop, each generation of school administrators must feel an obligation to leave a heritage of "good works" to its successors. This means a continuous program of inservice activities, varied in scope and comprehensive in nature, to meet more adequately the pressing demands of educational administration.

It will cost money to expand and increase the quality of professional growth opportunities at both national and state levels. It is strongly believed that much of this cost should be met by the members of the profession through dues or fees. The rationale for this belief rests upon the conviction that a person values a growth experience or enrichment if it has come at some personal sacrifice. A true profession cannot be built with wishful thinking or through mere mechanical manipulations. Here, as in all other truly worthwhile cultural achievements, the deeper feelings and the spirit of the creator must be imparted into the creation. It is only as men and women give of themselves and of their substance that real contributions will be made to the profession of school administration. That which is done at little cost of human time and effort will be regarded lightly and, perhaps, be of little consequence. Institutions, organizations, and professions that deeply affect the lives of people have not, in past history, grown up overnight like mushrooms after a warm summer shower. Nor are they likely to grow up and substantially add to their maturity in such fashion in the future. It is contended here that as the quality of professional growth activities and the inservice enterprise becomes more significant, varied, and worthwhile, participants will need to and be willing to pay a higher price for it.

On the other hand, it is only reasonable to assume that financial support for larger research projects undertaken by national and state associations should come from foundations or tax sources. Local boards of education can and should be requested to increase their support of specialized workshops, institutes, and seminars designed to upgrade the competencies and skills and to add to the knowledge of various groups of administrators and supervisors within their school systems. A distinction should be made between professional growth activities designed for individual improvement and those intended to benefit groups of administrators and the total process of school administration in the local district. The cost of the former should be borne, in large part, by the individual and by the professional organizations which he supports; the latter, by funds supplied by boards of education, state educational agencies, and tax-supported institutions of higher education.

Up to this point in this discussion, the case for an improved program of professional growth activities for educational administrators has been made in general terms. But proposals that have promise for being accepted and implemented in action programs must be specific where specificity is necessary. The roles of the American Association of School Administrators and the state associations need to be spelled out in greater detail and in more specific terms.

## The Role of AASA

As the program of leadership services of the American Association of School Administrators is projected into the immediate future, strengthening the profession of school administration and improving the capabilities of individual administrators will undoubtedly be given high priority. There are many approaches that may be made toward accomplishing this purpose.

1. A continuing inservice education committee composed of individual administrators from the profession who have demonstrated both knowledge and skill in some particular area or aspect of educational administration should be established.

2. An increase in AASA Headquarters staff should be made to provide more full-time leadership personnel for expanding the program of services.

3. A roster of "specialists" in the membership should be compiled. Undoubtedly, there are many members in AASA who have clearly demonstrated a special knowledge or skill in some phase of educational administration. These people should be more widely known so that they can be called upon by colleagues and groups of people to assist in local and state efforts to carry forward professional growth activities.

4. Promotion of high ethical standards is a professional responsibility at all levels. The national association can be of tremendous help to state and local groups of administrators in the development of ethical standards and securing of their common acceptance.

5. More research information is needed. AASA is not set up to conduct extensive research, nor does it have the resources. However, as a part of a comprehensive inservice program, it can serve a useful purpose in stimulating research, calling attention to problems that ought to have priority in research programs, and disseminating research findings. A special committee could meet from time to time

and, by means of a special report or other media of communication, call attention to research needed in school administration. This committee would not need to limit its thinking and planning to the manipulatory problems of administration. In addition to problems of this nature, it could extend its explorations to include instructional methods, human relations, school facilities, and the intricate processes of learning.

6. Summaries of research and studies should be more widely publicized and the number of such publications increased. Cooperation with Syracuse University, which led to making available to every member of AASA the monograph, *Schoolmen and Politics,* a report of the extensive research project carried on in the Northeastern part of the United States by Stephen K. Bailey,[2] is an example of how the Association can assist in bringing pertinent research findings to school administrators.

7. National and regional inservice activities for which the membership expresses a need and a demand should be expanded. When needs are clearly defined and there is a demand from the membership that they be met, the Association should have financial resources and personnel to meet them. Otherwise, there is but little point in further projection of the inservice function of the Association.

8. Closer liaison with educational institutions is necessary. It is very important for the profession to keep abreast of developments in the training and preparation of administrators and supervisors. The seminar for professors of school administration conducted by the American Association of School Administrators at the University of Nebraska in 1962 is an excellent example of a practical step that can be taken in developing and maintaining closer working relationships between professors of school administration and school superintendents.

The list of suggestions given above is not intended to be exhaustive. Rather, it is intended as an illustration of the kinds and qualities of activities that are appropriate and that all administrators in the country can fruitfully engage in through their national organization to make educational administration the responsible force in this country that it can be.

In looking forward with a long-range view to an inservice program for school administration, the members of the American Association of School Administrators, individually and collectively, should direct their attention to the purposes and values that undergird public education and to the moving forces that bear upon administrative decision and action at almost every point, as well as to the operational procedures for mobilizing

---

[2] Bailey, Stephen K., and others. *Schoolmen and Politics.* Syracuse, N.Y.: Syracuse University Press, 1962. 111 pp.

physical and human resources and bringing them to bear at points in the educational enterprise when and where they are needed. Assessment of the findings of research designed to reveal deficiencies in school administration strongly suggests that the need for school administrators to be well informed on broad cultural issues and to comprehend the life of their communities in totality becomes more urgent year after year.

Strong leaders from labor, business, industrial, and civic organizations and from the different political groups with whom superintendents work in their communities in shaping the educational program for the school district are well acquainted with the seriousness of issues before the country and are aware of the implications of these issues for the particular segments of the culture with which they are most vitally concerned. Each and all of these leaders have facts, have opinions, have beliefs, and have prejudices. The superintendent must work with all of them. And he must meet them with confidence, with professional dignity, and on equal footing. To assist administrators in meeting this important challenge day after day and month after month is an important function of an inservice program for school administration. It is part of the image of an inservice program that the professional association must conceptualize, project, and support until it becomes an accepted part of the ongoing process of developing and supporting educational leadership.

## The Role of State Associations

State associations of school administrators have equally important roles to perform, not in the sense of duplicating, but of supplementing, national efforts. Due to variations in organization and structure, it is difficult to define these roles.

State-wide efforts to promote the professional growth of educational administrators may be centered around institutions of higher learning, or states may be divided into geographical districts or regions for the purpose of better serving their members. When large cities exist in a state, inservice programs to meet the needs and interests of administration are almost invariably developed in the metropolitan area. Regardless of how the state association is structured or how state efforts are organized, the administrators, acting together through their professional state organization, should plan, organize, and sustain a continuous program for their own professional improvement.

There is, of course, no one pattern of organization or series of activities that will be suitable and workable in all states. Such uniformity would be totally out of harmony with the principles of good educational planning. But, as points of departure, state associations should give careful thought to—

1. Establishing an advisory committee comprised of representatives from boards of education and citizens groups having an interest in and a desire to increase the competence of educational administrators. Each member of the advisory committee should have demonstrated competence in some area of school administration or should have a keen interest in the improvement of the profession.

2. Making resources available for providing leadership assistance and financial support to local, district, or regional groups desiring to initiate and to develop inservice projects and activities. It is fully recognized that such support will result in higher dues for members, but there is good reason for believing that as greater value is received from membership in the state association, increases in dues not only will be acceptable but will be encouraged by members.

3. Establishing regular study groups throughout the state, planned and located so that superintendents from "one-administrator" school systems will have opportunities to join with their colleagues in the consideration of common problems of school administration.

4. Developing a roster of resource persons from among the membership in the association. The intent of such a listing would be to make it easier to draw upon and utilize to better advantage the leadership potential of the state in an inservice program.

5. Maintaining a cooperative relationship with teacher education institutions. The purpose of these continuing working relationships would be to support, as well as to review critically, the preservice programs for educational administrators and supervisors and, at the same time, to utilize to better advantage the resources in these institutions in dealing with educational problems in local districts.

6. Serving as a clearinghouse for significant research in administration and for reporting pertinent action research in educational administration. This is a role state associations could well play, and such service is much needed in most states.

7. Expanding inservice programs for administrators to the point where leaders from business, industry, and government are willing and eager to share with superintendents their experiences in administration that have relevance to the problems and issues of school organization and management and assisting local school administrators and school systems in securing good consultative services. Strong associations in the larger states could and should provide some consultative services through full-time staff members. There are but few state associations that at the present time have full-time or even part-time staff members. However, there is a trend in this direction. During the years immediately ahead, state associations can be most helpful in developing criteria that should

be used in securing and using consultants and in calling attention to highly competent people in specialized fields.

8. Representing the profession at the state level when issues or matters having important implications for the profession are before the state legislature and state-wide groups and organizations.

9. Working for higher standards of professional performance in all phases of school administration. This is no simple undertaking, nor is it a task that will ever be completed. It calls for persistent effort toward the development of standards which, if adhered to, will raise the level of performance of administrators throughout the entire state.

10. Developing, gaining acceptance of, and enforcing a code of ethics for educational administrators. This is a task that should not be minimized or neglected. The ethics of school administration have but little worth or meaning except as they are embedded in the values of individuals and are truly reflected in the spirit of how they act and what they do. A code of ethics for school administration must be of the profession. It is not a body of rules of conduct that can be borrowed in times of emergency or imposed as a penalizing measure when decency and good taste are offended.

## Focal Points of Effort

In keeping with the basic values that undergird all American culture, the driving force behind the professional improvement of school administration rests in large measure with the individual. Professional improvement is made only as changes take place in individuals, only as they grow in understanding and in their ability to accept and to meet recurring responsibilities. Individual administrators, as has been pointed out, must combine their efforts in group activities, but, individually, they must give of themselves and be willing and ready to do a little bit more than that which is required of them. This extra effort is the margin of professional growth.

Inservice education is a rigorous process requiring independent thinking, self-discipline, and dedicated effort. Men and women seek to become more thoroughly acquainted with some special phases of educational administration, at the same time making doubly sure that they do not neglect the broader humanistic bases of professional work.

The school administrators of this country have committed themselves to upgrading and improving the profession to which they belong. They are not waiting to be pushed forward by directives from state boards of education or by legislative action. Rather, they have taken the initiative and are encouraging legislative enactment and the development of state boards of education and local district policies that would support and sustain the forward movement toward improving and strengthening the whole process of administration that they themselves have in large part generated through their own professional organizations. They are, so to speak, lifting themselves by their own bootstraps. Of course, they are not working alone. They are cooperating and working closely with state departments of education, colleges and universities, and local school boards. They are enlisting the support of great foundations and seeking assistance from business and industrial groups. The restless energy which moves this program forward is in evidence in every state, on every major university campus, in every state department of education, and in thousands of cities and towns and rural communities.

Ideas, beliefs, and concepts cannot be carried forward in abstraction. They are carried forward through projects and activities that give them meaning and substance. They become alive and take on cloaks of reality as something is done about a problem or an issue that is important to people. A large part of the leadership program of the American Association of School Administrators is of an inservice nature. The following highlights of the program over the past few years clearly suggest such emphasis:

1. Annual conventions of the Association at which administrators and other leaders discuss literally hundreds of educational problems and hear informative and stimulating speakers

2. Educational exhibits at the convention which bring to members of the Association up-to-date information on all types of materials, supplies, and equipment used in the schools

3. Publications of the Association which have dealt with such broad problems as school-plant planning, superintendent-school board relationships, staff relations, curriculum, citizenship, public relations, and school district reorganization

4. Architectural exhibits at the convention which bring to the members new and fresh ideas on school-plant planning

5. Drive-in conferences in which superintendents and other educational leaders come together in various parts of the country to think through practical down-to-earth problems of educational administration

6. The Educational Research Service which makes available to the membership objective information about current school problems

7. The Educational Policies Commission (jointly supported with the National Education Association) which, over a period of 25 years, has carefully formulated policy statements that have been widely circulated and have had a vital influence in shaping the ongoing course of public education in this country

8. The Cooperative Program in Educational Administration which has been sustained over a period of 15 years and which has undoubtedly been the most concentrated and most effective effort that the Association has made toward upgrading the profession.

The programs of state associations differ from the national association program mainly in scope and degree. These associations have moved the profession forward through meetings, publications, research projects, study groups, and through cooperation with organizations and institutions in their respective states. Programs include activities and efforts for developing better understanding of the teaching-learning process, bringing about closer affinity between the schools and community life, cooperating with universities in strengthening preservice programs for school administration, improving local school district organization, lending their efforts to recruiting superior candidates for the profession of school administration, aiding in the development of case studies for the instruction of graduate students in school administration, and supporting internship programs.

As the leadership of the professional organizations continues to be exerted toward professional improvement, new approaches must be found for carrying ideas forward. There is no guarantee that what has worked well in the past will prove to be adequate for the future. Mark Twain is reputed to have said that the best education he received came from his experience as an apprentice pilot on the Mississippi River. After he had learned all the shoals and points on the river from St. Louis to New Orleans, he found on his next trip that many of them had changed, and he had to learn them all over again. Such is the challenge and the task for the state associations and the national association of school administrators as they lend their efforts to developing and sustaining inservice programs that will adequately meet the needs of the times.

# CHAPTER ELEVEN

# Resources Essential for an Inservice Program

$\mathbf{T}$HE resources essential for initiating and sustaining an effective inservice program for school administration are many and varied. They include such intangibles as positive and forward-looking attitudes on the part of people involved, a climate of mutual respect and confidence between those who receive services and those who provide them, well-formulated policies developed and clearly stated by controlling agencies and institutions, and an operational plan of action. And they require substantial financial resources and countless hours of careful work by skilled people. Institutes, workshops, study groups, conferences, planning activities, research, and publications cannot be had for the asking.

As in any other endeavor or enterprise, resources for an inservice program for school administration must be mobilized in some fashion. For the most part, this has been done in the past, and perhaps will continue to be done in the future, by state departments of education, institutions of higher education, professional associations, intermediate units of school administration, local districts, and individual administrators. While not all of the resources that are currently being used for the improvement of school administration in this country have been or can be brought together in operational centers, the principles of good administration demand that they be mobilized in a manner which permits their ready and efficient use.

To determine the financial contributions currently being made to inservice programs is not a simple matter. Specifically designated appropriations for inservice activities do not frequently appear in the budgets of local districts, state departments of education, and colleges and universities. And when they do appear, there tends to be an overlapping of services so that the contributions made to upgrading and improving school administration are difficult to distinguish. It is equally difficult to project a hypothetical budget for such purposes. Furthermore, it would be unsound to do this until the program is spelled out in some detail. Budgetary planning for inservice programs, like budgetary planning for any other educational activity, should be in terms of the program to be supported. The program comes first, and the budget supports it. Superintendents have vigorously supported this procedure in all other phases of educational planning, and should continue to support it here.

### Specific Examples

In trying to comprehend the magnitude and variety of resources needed to support and sustain an inservice program for school administration, specific examples drawn from actual operations will undoubtedly be helpful. The illustrations which follow could be multiplied a hundredfold by drawing on the inservice programs of local school districts, intermediate districts, state departments of education, state associations of school administrators, and nearly every major college and university in the country.

### Cooperative Programs in Educational Administration

Over a period of 15 years, the Kellogg Foundation has liberally supported the development of comprehensive preservice and inservice programs through which the school superintendents and principals of this country have added to the storehouse of information and skills needed in their complex work.

The first phase of this dynamic professional movement was termed the Cooperative Program in Educational Administration (CPEA). With coordination through the CPEA, approximately 140 of the nation's institutions of higher education cooperated with the eight key university centers. State departments of education, local-state-national professional associations, hundreds of schoolboards, and many citizens encouraged the in-service education of thousands of public school leaders. After 1955 there was a change in the focus of the program, it subsequently centering upon an intensification relating to those problems revealed to be the most significant and difficult of solution during the initial five years. The Foundation has been a collaborator through its grants totaling nearly seven million dollars to the participating institutions and agencies over the decade.[1]

The contributions to this nationwide program for improving school administration made by universities, state departments of education, local school districts, professional associations of school administrators, and individuals who have been personally involved have without question exceeded many times the contributions of the Foundation. While much of

---

[1] W. K. Kellogg Foundation. *Report for 1960.* Battle Creek, Mich.: the Foundation, 1960. p. 39.

the expenditure of time and money in this program has been devoted to preservice preparation, there is scarcely any part of it that has not had implications of an inservice nature. The research findings have been as useful to men and women on the job as they have been to the students who are yet looking forward to becoming administrators.

Many of the graduate students who engaged in the advanced study programs in universities and brought distinction to themselves, to the university in which they worked, and to the total profession were recruited from responsible administrative positions. Specific attacks were made on practical problems again and again, and superintendents, together with their boards, have been involved in a countless number of institutes, workshops, conferences, and other inservice activities. The amendment to the AASA Constitution that set two years of professional preparation beyond the bachelor's degree in an accredited institution as a prerequisite for active membership in the Association is convincing evidence of the influence this program has had on the total profession.

*AASA Inservice Activities*

A more intimate understanding of costs of an inservice program can be obtained by looking at budgetary appropriations for specific AASA activities. These items, quoted from a letter written by Finis E. Engleman, November 21, 1961, clearly indicate that AASA's support of the professional improvement of the school superintendency is not limited to well-wishing and a kindly, paternalistic interest.[2] This program is supported through appropriations in the 1962 budget of the Association as follows:

| | |
|---|---|
| Inservice education project | $5,000 |
| Drive-in conferences | 5,000 |
| State presidents meeting | 17,000 |
| Support of NCATE | 2,000 |
| High horizons seminars | 1,500[3] |
| Travel to state association meetings | 2,250 |
| Support of a joint committee with the National Association of Secondary-School Principals, the Department of Elementary School Principals, the Association for Supervision and Curriculum Development, and AASA for preliminary planning on standards for preparation programs | 600 |

[2] Letter from Finis E. Engleman to Maurice F. Seay, November 21, 1961.
[3] Actual expenditures amounted to approximately $4,500.

Publication on superintendent-school board relations                 3,000

Publication of *School District Organization*                        3,200

Publication of research report, *Profiles of the School Superintendent*                                              5,000

Publication of *Stateside,* a pamphlet prepared especially for leaders of state associations                         2,000

It should be pointed out that these are items of expenditure in a relatively small budget. Furthermore, they do not reflect the cost of staff time that was devoted to these activities and represent only a part of AASA's inservice program. It can almost be said that everything the Association does—its annual convention, its publications, its Educational Research Service, and the many conferences and institutes in which it participates throughout the year—is part of a comprehensive professional improvement program. However, these specific items do suggest the necessity for dollar-and-cents appropriations behind inservice activities.

*Drive-in conferences.* For the past 15 years, the American Association of School Administrators has joined with the Department of Rural Education of the NEA (with the Council of Chief State School Officers serving as a cosponsor) in sponsoring a series of regional drive-in conferences. The programs for each of these conferences are planned by a committee of superintendents representing the states in the region where each conference is held. The budgetary appropriations of the associations are sufficient to meet the cost of the initial planning committee meetings and to bear the expense of printing conference programs and securing speakers.

A member of the AASA staff and a member of the Department of Rural Education staff meet with these planning committees to plan the programs and invariably attend and take part in the conferences. Actual leadership responsibility for managing the conference is delegated to the planning committees. The total cost is shared equally by the Department of Rural Education and AASA. Over this long period of time in which approximately 75 different conferences have been held, the average cost to AASA has been about $1,000 per conference. The cost to the Department of Rural Education has been, of course, about the same. In addition to the expenditures of these associations, school boards, colleges and universities, state departments of education, and individual superintendents have met the cost incurred in attending these meetings.

Again, this is an example of how a small amount of resources provided and used cooperatively goes a long way in initiating and sustaining a worthwhile inservice program. But, again, it must be pointed out that some financial resources *are* needed to get such programs off the ground and keep them going.

## A University Conference

For the past 20 years, Teachers College, Columbia University, has been conducting an annual three-week work conference for school superintendents. The procedures used in organizing this conference are simple and direct. Letters of invitation are extended to 35 or 40 outstanding administrators representing school systems in almost every part of the country. Once superintendents have accepted the invitation to participate, follow-up letters are sent by the University to the respective boards of education, encouraging them to pay the cost of their superintendents' participation in this conference.

In a letter of invitation to superintendents for the 1962 conference, officials at the University pointed out that the conference fee would be $350 and estimated living expenses, $200, making a total cost of $550 per person involved in this well-known inservice activity.

## The Local School District

A decision by a local board of education to initiate and to support a substantial inservice program for school administration should not be interpreted to mean that the staff is poorly trained, inadequate, or inept, or that the board of education lacks confidence in it. To the contrary, it may well indicate recognition of potential that is only partially developed and creative abilities that are untapped and unused. Inservice programs may well begin after a strong staff is at work. The chances for fruitful returns from investment by a local district in an inservice program are likely to be as great or even greater if it has a highly trained and competent professional staff than if its staff is less capable.

Policies established by boards of education that support inservice programs are frequently broad and designed to encourage professional growth on the part of all employees in the district while concentrating mainly on the administrative personnel. In working through the problems that confront him and becoming better acquainted with the forces that play upon the organization and operation of the schools, the administrator sees the problems before him in better light, and better ways of operation frequently are found. Funds provided to bring consultants to work with staff members in refining and improving instructional practices may well be as effective in furthering the professional growth of administrators as they are in improving teacher effectiveness.

In a specific instance, a large school system with an enrollment of over 95,000 pupils, more than 100 schools, and a professional staff of about 4,000 people has worked closely over a period of years in cooperation with a nearby university in a continuous inservice program for strengthening administrative leadership in the school system. In this instance, budgetary appropriations and staff assignments provide opportunities for six carefully selected junior administrators to devote their full time to on-the-job learning for one year as a part of an internship program.

The regular salaries of these interns, not to exceed $7,725, are paid in full. All but $1,000 per intern is paid by the local district. This $1,000 per intern is paid by the university. In return, the university receives one full day of work per week from the intern, who serves as a student assistant to one or more faculty members of the university. This district invests $50,000 each year in this program. In addition to these financial resources, substantial contributions are made in staff time of top-level administrators and supervisors in the system who guide and direct the work of the interns. One top-level professional staff member is specifically designated to work with these interns.

The university assigns one staff member to work on a one-fourth, part-time basis with these interns. His time is devoted to individual consultation, group conferences, planning individual programs of activities, and evaluation. This university staff member accepts this responsibility as a major part of his assignment from the school of education.

Numerous examples of a comparable nature could be cited wherein local school districts are making substantial financial investment in developing administrative leadership for their school systems. Where such policy has been adopted, it is based upon the belief that this is one of the most economical and sensible approaches that can be made by a local board of education to add additional measures of quality to the instructional program in its school system.

Inservice programs for administration in local districts do not just happen. Provisions are made to—

1. Identify objectives.
2. Plan both immediate and long-range activities leading toward accomplishing established objectives.
3. Assign time for all individuals concerned, including appropriate inservice training units within personnel divisions in larger school districts.

4. Budget sufficient funds on a continuing basis for this phase of district research and development.
5. Establish and maintain an adequate district professional library to supplement the specialized resources of individuals in the district.
6. Encourage the staff by advancing those qualified to more demanding positions as opportunities occur within or outside the district.
7. Authorize short-term leaves and longer-term sabbatical leaves with partial salary to provide inservice growth opportunities outside the district of employment.

## The Intermediate District

The well-organized, well-staffed, and well-supported intermediate district of school administration is able to extend to smaller school systems inservice opportunities that are seldom provided outside of larger well-administered local districts. Through pooling personnel and fiscal resources, it develops sufficient strength at the intermediate district level to support strong programs. The very fact that the intermediate district, by its nature, must lead rather than direct creates a situation in which programs must be good. If they are not really worthwhile, they are ignored and may even be treated with disdain by local district personnel.

The intermediate district of school administration in California is a notable example of a well-organized and well-supported leadership unit. In this state, a county school service fund amounting to approximately $3.70 per pupil in average daily attendance is allocated by the state to the intermediate district office as a part of the state school financial support plan. These funds which come from the state directly to the county intermediate district superintendent's office constitute an important part of the intermediate district budget. Furthermore, school laws in this state make it permissible for local districts, through contractual arrangements with the county superintendent's office, to purchase services from the intermediate district. With these additional funds made available through such contractual arrangements, high-quality professional people are employed to serve the local districts in proportion to the amount of their contributions. This is an illustration of a cooperative arrangement made possible through the intermediate district.

Many intermediate districts in California budget as much as one-fifth of the total time of the professional staff. They provide the leadership for special staff meetings and conferences throughout the county; conduct seminars, workshops, and institutes; and maintain continuity in the operation of county school administration and county school board association work. Funds are also available through the intermediate district office to bring consultants from other systems in the state, from university campuses, and from outside the state to work with local district personnel in advancing special projects. The following excerpts from the Los Angeles County *Administrative Policies and Procedures Handbook* indicate the purpose and the character of the intermediate district program. The leadership and service program of this intermediate district, which may differ in detail, but not generally in purpose, from any other intermediate district, is developed in keeping with the belief that the intermediate district should—

1. Give support to and assist local school districts on the one hand and the State Department of Education on the other.

2. Help each district to develop the highest possible degree of independence in the sense of local adequacy in organization and operation.

3. Help all districts within the county to develop the optimum degree of interdependence and cooperation for their mutual benefit.

4. Cooperate with the California State Department of Education in developing the optimum degree of interdependence among the counties of the state for their mutual benefit.

5. Seek to improve the working relationships of the schools of the Los Angeles area with other organizations and agencies serving children and youth.

6. Provide leadership on the growing edges of educational development.

7. Provide assistance without interference and leadership without domination.

8. Through its ways of working (internally, with districts, and with other agencies or organizations), serve as an example of highly developed democratic procedure.

9. Conceive of its functions in terms of these principles and continually work at the state, county, district levels for improved ways of performing its emerging functions and its operations in the best possible manner.[4]

Funds are specifically earmarked for activities of an inservice nature through the county superintendent's office in California in the following proportions:[5]

---

[4] Los Angeles County Schools. *Administrative Policies and Procedures Handbook.* Los Angeles: Board of Education, 1960. pp. 3-4.

[5] Letter from T. Stanley Warburton to Shirley Cooper, August 15, 1962.

| Most Recent Annual Average Daily Attendance in the County | Maximum Amount per Average Daily Attendance |
|---|---|
| 0 — 9,999 | $ .050 |
| 10,000 — 14,999 | .045 |
| 15,000 — 24,999 | .040 |
| 25,000 — 49,999 | .035 |
| 50,000 — 99,999 | .030 |
| 100,000 and over | .025 |

County offices in California, with the help of special service funds, bring extension courses and special consultants from universities and colleges to local districts. There is considerable cost in administrative overhead in establishing inservice instructional college opportunities which are rightfully provided for in the intermediate district budget. Some counties have found it necessary and advantageous to underwrite workshops to the extent of 50 percent of the cost, with the local districts assuming the other half of the cost. Specialists from county staffs also contribute to the growing number of seminars operated by local school districts for potential school administrators. Both time and funds are required for such activity.

The professional library is another important adjunct of the county intermediate district office. Budget requirements for personnel, housing, and materials essential in maintaining and operating the library are substantial and must be provided for on a continuing basis for effective service.

Annual reports with adequate background material cost money, but should be provided by the county intermediate district for the use of administrators as well as for the information of the general public. These documents are extremely useful in interpreting historic trends, projecting future needs, developing understanding of the complex operation of the school districts, and interpreting school laws and policies pertaining to the management and use of funds.

From a hasty review of several intermediate district leadership programs in California, the following inservice activities have come to attention:

1. Staff members spend four days of each week in the field working with local school district personnel on a wide variety of educational problems. Friday is reserved for a staff meeting and a program which usually includes a seminar, with staff members analyzing educational problems and issues.

2. A county-wide workshop developed with the cooperation of the administrators of the several local districts in the county is held each year. In this workshop, attention is directed toward innovations

in the instructional program and broad problems of concern to all districts.

3. The assistant superintendents from the elementary school districts meet monthly with representatives of the intermediate district staff to work on curricular problems.

4. The assistant superintendents from secondary school districts and principals of secondary schools meet monthly with members of the intermediate district staff to think through instructional problems. The program for these meetings are planned well in advance. The data and other materials presented are carefully prepared.

5. Workshops are held in each of the local districts in the county. The county intermediate district underwrites 50 percent of the cost of each of these workshops. Professors from a nearby state college serve as leaders and consultants in each workshop.

6. The county intermediate district supports an inservice program for assistant deans of the larger high schools in the county.

7. The intermediate district supports an ongoing inservice program in which administrators as well as teachers study new developments in the teaching of arithmetic.

These examples of inservice education activities are a few of the many illustrations that could be called to attention in which the time of intermediate district personnel and the financial resources of the intermediate district are used in professional improvement programs.

## State Departments of Education

It is difficult to identify dollars-and-cents expenditures with specific leadership activities of state departments of education as they carry forward an inservice program such as has been described in Chapter 9. There is overlapping, of course, at every point with every function of the departments.

## Colleges and Universities

Until inservice education is fully accepted as a function of colleges and universities and this responsibility is truly reflected in operational policy in the employment and assignment of faculty members, in the development of research programs, and in budgetary planning, the services of many colleges and universities to school administration will tend to be incidental, accidental, and not well organized. The resources that will be needed as better programs emerge will, for the most part, be in terms of staff time and financial support. Much of the financial resources allocated for this purpose will be used in making the leadership potential that exists in the staff available at the time and at the place needed.

The following excerpt from a descriptive report of an inservice program at Auburn University illustrates clearly and forcefully the step-by-step procedures that were followed by the leaders in this institution and superintendents in neighboring school districts in blending policy, staff time, and financial resources into an effectively operating inservice program.

For years, colleges of education have claimed as a primary objective the up-grading of instructional programs in public schools within their area of contact and influence. Public schools have applauded the acceptance of this responsibility by colleges. They have, in turn, accepted the fact that success in their efforts toward continuous improvement of their instructional programs is dependent upon the degree to which available human and material resources are identified and utilized, especially what colleges of education have to offer.

Yet this alignment of purposes between colleges of education and public school systems has not been especially rewarding. This common objective has been restricted by continuation of separate and insular patterns of operation by the two groups. Colleges have, in the main, continued to operate programs and services primarily in terms of their perceptions of school needs, on something of a "take it or leave it" basis. Some progress has been made by gearing summer school calendars to public school calendars, offering extension courses, and designing courses to promote action research of a practical nature. Consultative services have been made more accessible and perhaps more effective. Still, the tendency has continued for the college to view its program and services from the secure and comfortable ivory tower, coming down for more effective and realistic views in few and isolated instances.

Similarly, public school personnel have continued to experience difficulties in making maximum use of college resources in improving instruction. Although teachers and administrators have enrolled in colleges for further professional training in increasing numbers, they have done so perhaps more for salary and certification rewards than for the contributions such further study could make to their improved competencies. Indeed, prevailing criticisms by public school personnel are that, "College courses are too theoretical and philosophical"; "They do not deal with practical problems I face every day"; and "What the professor says sounds good, but it won't work in the classroom." The recency of the college professor's experience in the public school classroom and thus his awareness of and competence in solving instructional problems are questioned also.

Most schools today profess to have in-service education programs, and there seems to be an increased tendency for college staff members to assist in those programs. Yet it seems that most such participation is generally viewed by both college and public school people as being only partially effective. Public school people often feel that what the professor says and does is impractical. The professor often feels his hands are tied when he is asked to "come out" only a few times a year, and then his responsibility is too often one of "talking about guidance." There seems to be no shortage of willingness or effort by either party, since mutual objectives and responsibilities for instructional improvement have been accepted. Nevertheless, an effective framework for working together on mutually accepted objectives is yet to be found. It may be on the horizon.

The problems and inadequacies described above were in the minds of the administration and staff of the School of Education at Auburn University in 1956 when careful study was made to assess the status of the School of Education and to project the role it should play in helping upgrade education in the State and region. From this study emerged a realization of the need to render improved services of a broader nature. A plan was soon developed which proposed to restructure existing relationships between the School of Education and the public schools of the State and region. This plan recognized the need to render services designed to assist public school inservice programs.

Efforts toward establishing a new relationship with public schools were greatly increased in June, 1957. Twenty newly elected superintendents responded favorably to an invitation to attend a conference at Auburn University to look together at the jobs they were about to assume and to consider the feasibility of initiating a continuous and cooperative working relationship between their school systems and the School of Education. The group identified common bonds and decided to organize around these bonds a continuing program for the purpose of exploring ways and means of improving instruction in the 20 school systems represented. The School of Education agreed to seek financial assistance for the new venture and assigned personnel to work in the program. Thus was born in this two-day meeting the Cooperative Program for Instructional Improvement.[6]

Inservice education merges with almost everything else that the state department does, as it provides leadership in developing policy and in giving direction to a state-wide educational program.

Activities that have implications for inservice education programs for school administrators are intermingled with inservice education of teachers and supervisors and with the working relationships of state department personnel with boards of education and with lay citizens. Even the research service that provides information about educational problems to school superintendents provides the same information to everyone else in the state who is interested. This is as it should be. It would be unfortunate if leaders in the profession, in their zeal to further improve the inservice program, cast it in the light of something that stands separate and apart from the total educational enterprise—something that is tacked on, something that is done to people rather than with and for people. Even with all of these complexities and interrelationships, Finis E. Engleman, a veteran chief state school officer with many years of experience, estimated that, during his term of office, three-fourths of the state department budget was spent on activities that directly or indirectly had some measure of value for the professional growth and improvement of school superintendents. Resources needed for initiating and sustaining an inservice program at the state level include adequate manpower, sufficient ongoing budgetary support, discerning publications, suitable housing available for ready use by people from the field, and adequate travel provision to enable leadership to go both to the field and to the places where broad points of view and specialized information can be obtained.

---

[6] Prepared by Robert L. Saunders, associate professor of education, and Ray Phillips, assistant professor of education, Auburn University, Auburn, Alabama.

Relations between state departments of education and local administration must be close, mutually trustful, and dynamic. Changes in the state of California were so dramatic during the decade following World War II that a major committee was appointed to study the "proper role and relationship of the state, county, and local district in public education in California." The work of this committee led to the establishment of the California Commission on Public School Administration. This commission issued *School Administration in California—A Pattern for the Future*, which since 1956 has served as a guide for improving administrative organization and relationship on all levels. In this official publication, the state agency for public education is recognized as existing to discharge a primary function of educational leadership. The five major aspects of the leadership are (a) planning, (b) research, (c) advising and consulting, (d) coordinating, and (e) public relations.

Recognition that leadership does not mean authoritarianism places heavy responsibility upon the state agency for helping to develop administration in the intermediate and local units adequate to perform their functions in an effective and appropriate manner. This is accomplished in large measure by example. The relationship between the state superintendent and the superintendent of the smallest district in the state may well condition the relationship between school administrators and classroom teachers and between classroom teachers and pupils in many large, populous school districts.

In exercising leadership, state agencies frequently convene meetings involving school staff and constituents who help with planning and coordinating administration and have major responsibility for the improvement of instruction. The preplanning of meetings, with the assistance of steering committees, frequently has more value for the participants, in terms of inservice growth, than do the larger and more formal state conferences, workshops, and conventions. Those involved in such planning are required to report areas of greatest need for information and inspiration. They must work with state leaders in selecting participants who can contribute to the growth of their colleagues. They have a responsibility for communicating to their peers the availability of this specialized training opportunity. And after the meetings have been held, they are among the persons who make the most discerning evaluation and report on the effectiveness of the activity to those responsible in state departments as well as in local and intermediate districts. They also have responsibility for maintaining continuity in the meetings of an organization. Their experiences as teachers have made them know that planned repetition is necessary for effective learning. Increasingly, the reporting of information from such meetings through publications or through electronic media is making them increasingly valuable to administrators in school districts where lack of resources make personal participation impossible.

The position of the state agency primarily as a policy-shaping body emphasizes the need for minimizing its regulatory function and strengthening its leadership role. Staff organization and recruitment on the state level should be directed to this end. There are many instances in which school administration in all school districts in the state has been strengthened through leadership from the state agency. State departments which are adequate for the future must command outstanding leaders who by example and precept will stimulate, inspire, and guide administrators throughout the state. This means a re-examination of salary schedules in state agencies, for outstanding administrators will rarely move to a position in a state department for a salary less than they are offered in intermediate and local districts.

State departments of education are increasingly providing funds to support internship programs which help prepare administrators for work in the field. Internship programs that are truly useful are something more than a series of related work experiences. They are truly instructional in nature—instructional to the point that the tasks performed at any given time are clearly related in the intern's mind to the best-known theory and practice. The operation of such programs draws upon staff time for consultation and conferences. In a very real sense, the individual with whom an intern works takes on the cloak of an instructor from beginning to end. Thus, financial appropriations must be liberally supplemented with the time of high-quality professional staff employees if the internship program fully meets the expectations of the profession. State department administration, in sponsoring internship programs, should seek to provide instructional work experience opportunities for students in the very forefront of the advancement of school administration—with state committees for the advancement of school administration in the different states, with state associations of school administrators, with the American Association of School Administrators, and with the University Council for Educational Administration, as well as with the operational programs in local and intermediate district school systems.

### State Associations

The leadership of state professional organizations is severely handicapped in nearly every state by lack of full-time personnel and limited financial resources. The extremely limited budgets supported by dues paid by individual members, institutional memberships, occasional profits on exhibits, and some foundation funds are hard pressed to sustain even meager leadership programs. Work of the associations is carried forward, in most cases, by the voluntary contributions of individual members who serve on committees, organize and plan programs, write and distribute bulletins, and represent the interests of school administrators in their respective states in numerous meetings. These personal contributions of individual members constitute by far the largest resource of state associations. The funds available do little more than serve as a nucleus around which association work develops.

Most state associations are taking steps to increase their budgets by raising membership dues. This is an encouraging trend, but the fact still remains that in smaller states where the membership of the associations will always be relatively small, substantial budgets cannot be developed if membership dues continue to be the primary source of income. In several states, substantial assistance is given to the state association of school administrators through the provision of part-time staff members assigned to the association by the state department of education or by the state education association. In other instances, universities cooperate with state associations of school administrators in developing workshops, institutes, and study conferences.

But in most states, there are no full-time or even part-time employed association personnel. The program is carried forward on a voluntary basis by men and women who have other commitments and can only give association work their attention in spare moments. Fruitful as all of these efforts are, they frequently fall short of utilizing the full leadership potential of the association. Finding resources to help state associations employ and utilize full-time executive secretaries is one of the most important needs in the whole program of professional improvement.

### The Individual

The recruitment, preparation, selection, and assignment of supervisory and administrative personnel is advancing to the point where inservice programs properly start at a more advanced level than was previously possible. With a steadily diminishing number of districts, competition for top positions is becoming stronger. The individual entering administration must bring with him both the ability and willingness to continue learning if he expects to make a worthy contribution to the profession. He or she should budget time in both work and personal life for reading and formal study, for visitation of other school systems, for workshop and conference learning, and for university course work.

The individual needs to budget funds for his inservice training. A personal library of periodicals, books, and reports is essential. Much professional association work is of more value to the individual than to the district for which he works. Even when a district reimburses an individual for conference expenses, there will be inevitable costs of a personal nature which the individual must meet.

Many individuals plan careers in administration which include successive yet sustained experience in smaller districts leading to administrative positions in larger systems. Others recognize the increasing specialization of school administration and gear both their initial preparation and inservice efforts toward instructional supervision, school finance, construction, public information, and personnel administration in large school systems. The price the family pays while the family breadwinner completes a graduate degree at a university is an important item in the total cost of an inservice program for school administrators.

The prime factors in an inservice program are organization, substance, meaning, and personal identity. The cultural forces that buffet and beat upon the individual school administrator as he works with a board of education, an instructional staff, and a community of people at times seem overpowering and overwhelming. In pessimistic moments, he may feel that his efforts are too weak and too frail to be of much consequence —that he might as well resign himself to drifting with the tides of the times. But these are no more than passing moods. He does not stand alone, nor should he feel that he does. It is within his power to join with his fellows in analyzing these forces whether they be of an economic, political, or social nature, in seeking to discover their true meaning, and in striving to utilize them in shaping policies and in moving the educational program forward. Such analysis requires that he make explicit judgments as well as decisions in terms of facts, theory, and values.

The line-up of a school administrator's problems—how he sees them, how he states them, and the priorities he gives them—whether he knows it or not, depends upon his conception of administrative theory, the methods he commonly employs, and the values to which he adheres. Faulty decisions are often made and shortsighted policy is often recommended because administrators are bogged down and almost choked with undigested facts. They have not had the time and are frequently lacking in the intellectual techniques needed to bring them into order, assimilate them, and see them in a total configuration. The compelling drive on the part of individual administrators to join with their colleagues in gaining these new powers and these broader perspectives is the basic resource in all inservice programs for school administration. To go back to a quotation from Ezra Cornell cited in an earlier chapter of this book, "There is not a single thing finished."

## To Move Ahead

Considerable effort and money will have to be expended by individuals, districts, county officers, state departments of education, colleges and universities, and professional associations before the kind of inservice programs envisioned by the Commission on Inservice Education are off the ground and under way. This nation is currently expending nearly $14 billion per year for research and development. Of this amount, $10 billion is being spent by industries whose leaders know full well that this is the only way to assure sound operation with attendant profit to stockholders. Governmental and other agencies are investing $4 billion per year for research and development. Careful study shows that all the agencies sharing a responsibility for research and development of educational administration have made only a modest beginning.

To move ahead in inservice education for school administration in a manner that is comparable to the efforts being made to add new dimensions of power to leadership capacities in other facets of the culture, objectives must be clearly stated, programs carefully delineated, and a financial plan developed to support the program. Such programs will be team operations in which there is flexibility and opportunity for individuals to make choices just as individuals choose the paths they follow and the purposes they pursue in other facets of American life.

The program may be simple in its approach as it supports administrators in their efforts to do a better job day after day. It will involve cooperation of people and pooling of resources in local districts and county and state agencies. It will draw upon assistance from national organizations and agencies, where circumstances permit. It will require the confidence of boards of education in their staff members and a willingness to provide the time and monetary support essential for sharing the know-how and knowledge required in an age in which culture changes so rapidly that one can rightly say of almost any operational technique that if it works it is already obsolete.

# In Perspective

$J$ONATHAN Swift, with truthful tongue-in-cheek, wrote many years ago:

> . . . geographers [who] in Afric maps
> With savage pictures fill their gaps,
> And o'er unhabitable downs
> Place elephants for want of towns.[1]

The Commission on Inservice Education, in what has gone before, has been saying that there are "gaps in *our* maps" for the totality of school administration in the United States. They have come because of people; they have arisen because of the times.

It has said that there is a firm, clear, and sweeping definition of school administration in which the superintendent is the central instrumentality, the personalization of the broad administrative function.

It has stated that there are startlingly new dynamics in the character of school administration; that growing processes of accelerated, endless change have been responsible for the increasing number of "map gaps."

The very dynamism of these processes, propelled by myriad movements in industry, business, science, social institutions, government, even religion, has been bringing cultural changes among our free people which bid fair to bring to actuality the very goals in an open society for which public education has struggled so long in this nation. The great and compelling task of public school administration, caught up in the heaving, weaving, and bobbing of these changes, is to prove equal to its major role in guiding the children and youth in the new liberties, responsibilities, and demands of this new age.

---

[1] Swift, Jonathan. "On Poetry, a Rhapsody." *Collected Poems of Jonathan Swift.* (Edited by Joseph Horell.) Cambridge, Mass.: Harvard University Press, 1958. Vol. 2, p. 746.

The basic purpose in this improvement of administration is to enable all school districts, large or small, to strengthen the leadership potential of the schools at all strategic points so that the program of the schools for the children can move forward and upward. Bringing about changes in people is the focal point in the organization and operation of an inservice program.

It was natural, therefore, to say that the initiation of inservice improvement for administrators must be simple and flexible; that planning must be jointly shared by those who receive and by those who extend the service; that the key role of finance for such a program must be so faced and solved that the school systems with the least resources and the greatest leadership needs can be as deeply involved in this continuous moving forward as the richest and largest school systems; that the program of improvement should be indigenous to the locality or area being served; that it must begin where people are, should be long range, and should enable them to go under their own power where they want to go; that the development of insights and understanding as to how administrative leadership can effect changes through group processes should be equal in importance to the development of know-how and technical skills; that inservice leadership personnel must be capable of inspiring, refreshing, and strengthening the administrative learners; that team spirit is essential throughout the entire hierarchical structure of the participating leadership; that this spirit should involve simplicity of organization and orientation; and that any inservice program must "stand up well under the rigid test of usefulness."

The Commission has learned that commendable islands of inservice activity for developing administrative leadership exist in many parts of the country. An island may be a university staff alert to the challenge of its opportunity; it may be a state department of education eager to reach beyond its legislatively mandated supervisory and implementation functions; or it may be a regional or state association of administrators or an intergroup effort on a regional level. Occasionally, there was evidence of associative school system dynamism in redefining today's administrative leadership demands.

All of this has led the Commission to reappraise the roles of the major bodies and groups who have an inescapable stake in the challenge to professional leadership in public education. Platitudes and clichés abound to support the thesis that everybody and every organization have a stake in this need. It is certainly true, to put it negatively, that "he who serves as his own lawyer has a fool for a client." It is also just as true, as Justice Holmes once wrote, that "general propositions do not decide concrete cases." Yet, between these polar opposites lies the problem of closing the gaps. Administrators, associations, preservice institutions, governments—everybody has this common problem.

In this connection, the Commission has said that colleges and universities have a responsibility for inservice training comparable to their responsibility for the preservice education of administrative leadership; that there is as great a challenge and opportunity for state departments to take up new tasks in on-the-job, administrative upgrading as there is for the local administrator to go beyond mere administrative routine and operational detail in the organization and execution of faculty meetings and work conferences; that all professional organizations, proliferating in numbers and kinds into specialties galore, have an exciting chance to join hands and move forward together into this new adventure; and that perhaps the key to unlocking a nationwide movement lies in the working together of the local superintendent and his board of education to lift all their sights to the true intellectual and emotional nature of leadership.

### Holism

It would appear from this recapitulation that there is need to express the noble concepts of professional words with plain language. Anything anybody in school administration in any way on any level does with or through anybody else at any time or any place in order to reach out individually and together in seeking new knowledge, new skills, or new insights will thereby enhance and enrich the public schools and their children. This would be in keeping with the totality of administration, in which the administrator plays a major role as part of a holism. If this is so, then there is need to describe the nature of the growth which, from time to time, will be appraised and about which judgments will be formed concerning the quality and extent of the progress being made.

### On Growing

The growth of an individual or a body of individuals does not make anyone different tomorrow or next year. Change is part of total change in the organism. It is adaptation and adjustment; it is not transmutation. Change is imperceptible at the time of its making, yet it becomes part of total growth, effected *into* the individual while subtly affecting all aspects and parts of the individual, thereby inducing change in previously unchanged parts of the organism. In this manner, human change and growth seek to overcome lopsidedness and outcroppings.

Growth, therefore, is a process of *becoming*.[2] It lies behind, beside, and beyond the individual. It is a restless mass of constant change, of creativity; it is what *is* happening to the individual as well as what *has* happened to him. Change, we too often mistakenly believe, is what remains after the scaffolding of courses, seminars, retreats, workshops, or problem units has been removed. Yet, in truth, change proceeds and moves into the structure while the scaffolding itself is rising. Take away the work scaffold, and what remains is a "finished" job which imperceptibly continues to change through deterioration, thereby requiring constant maintenance simply to remain "finished." As it is with school buildings, so it is also with school administration.

Growth is also *identification*. If the identification is healthy and sound, so will be the resulting growth. If the identification is imitative of unsoundness, growth again becomes deterioration. Thus, it is clear that identification as an aspect of growth is concerned with the self of the individual as it seeks not only itself but also the selves of all other individuals. Emerson made this abundantly clear on August 31, 1837, in his address to the Phi Beta Kappa Society at Cambridge. Preliminary to the body of his paper he discussed an old fable:

> ...[which] covers a doctrine ever new and sublime; that there is One Man— present to all particular men only partially, or through one faculty; and that you must take the whole society to find the whole man. . . . The fable implies that the individual, to possess himself, must sometimes return from his own labor to embrace all other laborers. But, unfortunately, this original unit, this fountain of power, has been so distributed to multitudes, has been so minutely subdivided and peddled out, that it is spilled into drops, and cannot be gathered. The state of society is one in which the members have suffered amputation from the trunk, and strut about so many walking monsters— a good finger, a neck, a stomach, an elbow, but never a man.
> Man is thus metamorphosed into a thing, into many things.
> In this distribution of functions the scholar is the delegated intellect. In the right state he is MAN THINKING. In the degenerate state, *when the victim of society*, he tends to become a mere thinker, or still worse, the parrot of other men's thinking.[3]

Growth, while it is the becoming process and projective identification, is also *exhilaration, vitalization*, and *invigoration*. This is to say that its process contains its own worth because it is satisfying to the individual in itself. By responding to the identification processes, it finds its own values, thus rising above and beyond itself and its previous climate. And

---

[2] Association for Supervision and Curriculum Development. *Perceiving, Behaving, Becoming: A New Focus for Education.* 1962 Yearbook. Washington, D.C.: the Association, a department of the National Education Association, 1962. p. 13.

[3] Emerson, Ralph Waldo. "The American Scholar." *The Complete Essays and Other Writings of Ralph Waldo Emerson.* (Edited by Brooks Atkinson.) New York: Modern Library, 1950. p. 46.

herein lies the magic whereby its own growth begets growth in other selves. And this is the beating heart of administration—receiving and giving in development and change.

### Evaluation—Process or Product?

If growth is not static, sporadic, or unilinear, then the appraisal of what *is* happening becomes more important than what *has* happened. If this is true, then evaluation is an integral part of the whole process of becoming.

A recent publication on this subject, concerning itself with the growth of children in the learning process, puts it this way: "Evaluation processes are significant factors in the development of the person who accepts and understands the process of becoming. . . . Evaluation should be a continuous examination of immediate experience rather than a procedure used at the end of a unit of work or at a specified time."[4]

The same work asserts the following:

The idea that the individual is the instrument and not the subject of becoming lends support to the efforts to shift the effort from evaluation by others to self-evaluation . . . . To become involved in self-evaluation, the learner must be willing to look at his experience honestly and without defense. Through action research the individual defines [his own] criteria for evaluating his effectiveness, collects evidence, and interprets its meaning. Self-evaluation also requires a trust in self; it is supported by the empathy and understanding of the. . .co-workers.[5]

Every individual caught up in the process of learning through self with other selves concurrently will sense his need to seek a wide range of individualized techniques and evidence to evaluate both himself and what is happening to him in the process of his learning. Almost unconsciously, he will begin to seek (a) original definition and repeated restatement or clarification of his objectives; (b) an assessment of his own knowledge and skills both before and after embarking upon a course of becoming something new, different, and better, and he will do this not only within himself as an individual but outside himself in contrast or comparison with others involved in the same processes; (c) further insight and understanding into his own motivations as self-growth evolves, which is simply another way of saying that evaluation is really an integral part of the growth or learning process; and (d) formal and ritualistic standards or criteria by which he can measure what is happening beyond him in the school system, thus to estimate the effectiveness of the motivations radiating from his own self-growth.

---

[4] Association for Supervision and Curriculum Development, *op. cit.*, p. 249.
[5] *Ibid.*

*Energizers—Transmitters—Producers*

To approach this task of administrative change and growth through individuals' working with and through each other in a planned program —a program shot through with continuous evaluation of happenings and changes—suggests that the self and group images beg for definition at the very start.

In the holistic concept of administration, the leadership function pre-eminently demands an energizer and will perish without one. This be-speaks a power source not in the structural setting of status, but rather in the life and growth-source sense. This means strength, vision, inspira-tion, solace, encouragement, self-denial, and a host of other qualities char-acteristic, in truth, of any master teacher who takes children as they are and opens the doors to enable them to move out into what they are capable of becoming. It is a role rather than an act.

This energizer will see himself as the very substance of all the humans who transmit his "growingness" into accompanying growth for others. He will perceive school directors as conductors of his power as they transmit their powers and abilities into an operational, policy-formulated framework by which and through which his strength and drive infuse the teaching body, collectively and individually. It is these teacher-transmitters who convey, each in his or her own way, the energy which makes an educational reality of the energizer through revitalized and quickened learning by the children. It is they who must carry the hallmark of the original leadership out into a strengthened nation of free, intelligent, capable, and productive citizens. Thus, and only thus, can the growth of the leadership self be finally evaluated, and evaluated it will be, in many practical ways—ways already being used to determine present short-comings and needs in just about every school system in the land.

*The Central Goal*

The central goal of growth is *quality,* a continuing and self-regenerat-ing newness in quality of teaching and learning because of quality in administration. This quality bespeaks a totality of performance that is communicated, understood, appreciated, and supported by the people whose children are being served.

Yet how can quality be evaluated? By organization, services, tracks, teams, television, taxes, transportation, staff, or by grouping, grading, nongrading, or what? No, and especially no, if the central theme of the Commission's report is that growth (and quality) comes through changes in people—all the people engaged in the educational enterprise.

Archibald B. Shaw came to this conclusion:

If there be a single test of quality in an educational institution, it is a lively dissatisfaction with things as they are and an active, open-minded search for ways to make them better. Where you find an administrator and teachers who are genuinely disturbed by their institution's shortcomings (and what one does perfectly fulfill its purpose?); who are studying new organization, new methods, new tools, new curriculum; who build a continuous measuring mechanism into their try-outs; who are fired with lively enthusiasm and warmed by a real concern for the people and purposes they serve; who are willing, while cheerfully granting to their colleagues the same right, to try out promising ideas without waiting to remake the whole school or convince the whole staff; there you may look for quality.[6]

If you will reread Shaw's conclusion, you'll see such words as *change, growth, becoming, process,* and *individual selves* peeking through almost every line, because it is in new quality that the process of becoming, the process of professional growth, begins to show itself. It can be evaluated continuously by its reaching out, ferment, experimentation, freedom and individuality, money sources for effecting the leadership growth, money sources for implementing that growing leadership, contagion and enthusiasm, and manysidedness.

## Divergent Roads

The Commission is persuaded that through the educational processes and the knowledge developed by and through the scholars who have sprung from free schools, the people of this country can command, direct, and utilize what they know to develop in a cooperative enterprise: the quality of leadership demanded by a time that will survive with nothing less. J. Robert Oppenheimer said it more eloquently:

I am aware of the difficulty of establishing in these fields (the social disciplines) rigorous criteria for competence and qualification. Nevertheless, at a time when the whole world realizes that many of its most vital problems depend upon an understanding of human behavior . . . and of the regularities which underlie the operations of our varied society, we should realize the great benefits which may come from attracting men and women of prominence to the study of these questions.[7]

Robert Frost has said the same thing many years earlier in his more simple and telling way:

> Two roads diverged in a yellow wood,
> And sorry I could not travel both
> And be one traveler, long I stood
> And looked down one as far as I could
> To where it bent in the undergrowth;

---

[6] Shaw, Archibald B. "The Measure of Quality." *Overview* 3: 11; January 1962.
[7] Oppenheimer, J. Robert. Quoted in Burton, W. H.; Kimball, R. B.; and Wing, R. L. *Education for Effective Thinking.* New York: Appleton-Century-Crofts, 1960. p. 364.

> Then took the other, as just as fair,
> And having perhaps the better claim,
> Because it was grassy and wanted wear;
> Though as for that the passing there
> Had worn them really about the same.
>
> I shall be telling this with a sigh
> Somewhere ages and ages hence;
> Two roads diverged in a wood, and I—
> I took the one less traveled by,
> And that has made all the difference.[8]

It is the individual and collective self continuously engaged in seeking this difference or differentness which will be the ultimate touchstone of evaluation.

### Viewed in Totality

All America has its eyes on the goal of an educational program that will be adequate to the age and to the problems confronting a dynamic culture. On a thousand different fronts, new sources of energy are being put into a total endeavor to bring public education in every city, village, and hamlet in the land to the point where it can meet the challenges of this age.

Inservice education for school administration is one of the points at which resources are being mobilized and used in bringing added vitality to the total educational program. As this program further develops, all who take part in it—all who have responsibility for shaping, supporting, and directing any of its aspects—have an obligation to scrutinize the results of their efforts in broad perspective and form opinions about the value of their efforts. This is the process of appraisal, of noting points at which progress has been made, of identifying limitations and shortcomings where they exist, of focusing attention on needs that yet remain unmet, and of balancing achievements against the efforts and resources which have been put into the program.

The ultimate test of usefulness of the inservice program will be the extent to which it has brought about better schools—richer and more varied opportunities for children to learn and grow, stronger and better-prepared teachers, more flexible school-plant facilities, and improvements at every point along the way toward the achievement of the educational program that is wanted and needed in this day and age.

---

[8] Frost, Robert. "The Road Not Taken." *The New Pocket Anthology of American Verse.* New York: Pocket Library, 1959. p. 201.

Citizens in school districts throughout the land will, in their own ways, form judgments about the usefulness of the inservice program. In this informal evaluation, opinions will be based upon specific observations about a particular aspect of the school program. These citizens will tend to judge the schools; the leadership in the school system; and, indirectly, the inservice program which supports this leadership in terms of what they in their totality have meant to them in a personal and individual way. These evaluations, in some measure, will reveal strengths and weaknesses and will focus attention on a superlative school system rather than on an outmoded school system. They will reveal strong spots and soft spots in the total educational program; and, at the same time, they will point out, in clear and dramatic fashion, accomplishments that the schools have made which are truly worthy of the great institution of public education. These evaluations, individually and collectively, will not directly and in specific fashion measure or make judgment about the quality, usefulness, and effectiveness of the inservice program. But, indirectly, they will appraise educational leadership in particular schools and in all public education. For, in the long run, it is what educational leaders do that determines, in large measure, the quality of the schools.

School board members, universities, and state departments of education that have supported inservice education programs in policy and devoted portions of their resources and measures of staff time to this end will view the inservice program for school administration in terms of administrative organization; in terms of educational policy that has been adopted by local school boards and that sustains and gives direction to educational programs; in terms of the holding power of individual schools; in terms of the extent to which outstanding teachers seek employment in one school system rather than in another located nearby; and in terms of the character of school-plant facilities and the professional stature of individual superintendents. In a word, these people who have had large measures of public trust for education bestowed upon them and, in keeping with their best judgment, have allocated a considerable proportion of the resources at their disposal to an inservice program for school administration cannot do otherwise than carefully scrutinize the results of their actions in such fashion. The acid test of the inservice program, as these responsible leaders review it in perspective, will be in the effect that it has had along the growing edge of the total educational program. For it is here that leadership meets the challenges of the times or falls short of expectations at crucial points.

The individual school administrator will view the inservice program in a personal manner. Having given of his time and effort and devoted

substantial financial resources to participating in this and that aspect of
the program, in the quiet of his office or in his home when there is time
for reflection, he will soberly ask if the program has been worthwhile;
if it has helped him find solutions to the difficult problems that confronted
him; if it has given him new insights and enabled him to work more
effectively with his school board, the members of his staff, and people in
the community; if, through it, he has gained a better understanding of
how children learn and grow mentally, emotionally, and physically; if
he has better understood and can utilize to better advantage the materials, techniques, and research findings that are a part of an ongoing
educational program; and if, as a result of the inservice program for
school administration, the schools for which he is responsible are a little
better than they would otherwise have been.

While the burden of evaluating inservice education for school administration falls primarily on the individual, it must be carried in no small
part by the total profession. No administrator stands entirely alone. He
has a kinship with all other administrators. He is a part of all that happens in the leadership, organization, and management of the schools.
Every notable accomplishment in the field adds, in some measure, to his
stature; and, conversely, he must carry his proportionate share of the
shortcomings and failures of his fellow administrators. Through sharing
experiences, pooling talents and resources, and cooperative effort at all
levels in all agencies and institutions and in all professional groups,
the image of the profession of school administration—its standards of
preparation and performance, its excellence and its ethics—is cast upon
the total cultural scene. Through what they do and how they perform
month after month and year after year, through the ideals to which they
adhere, and through the goals they set, administrators individually and
collectively are engaged in the never-ending task of developing a profession. As the profession sets its standards, so must it judge the inservice education program in terms of the contribution it makes toward
reaching them.

The really significant evaluations of the schools' responses to the
stimuli of the sixties, however, will be made by those community, state,
and national leaders who, by vested interest or legislative mandate, are
in a position to help or harm the total development of public education.
Thus far, too often, their evaluations have revealed dividedness, ex-
pediency, and lack of clear understanding of the role of public education
in a democratic society. These evaluations have shown up as judgments
in legislative halls, in school board meetings, and in expressions of
opinions through mass media of communication. They have emerged in

recent literature, too, in the caricatures of John Hersey's *Child Buyer,* Vance Packard's *Status Seekers,* and many others.

Yet today's times, while more dynamic than even the first half of the twentieth century, bear a strong similarity to a more distant past. Wickersham wrote in 1886 about conditions in the 1850's in Pennsylvania's county school systems:

> While the ill feeling toward the office lasted, the County Superintendents, in performing their work, had to row against a strong, rough tide. Their examinations were often unjustly criticized, their visitations were unwelcome, their advice was unheeded, and even their presence was considered an offense. Under these circumstances, the weak did nothing, the timid shrunk from the conflict, and none but the strong and brave could make a fight with any hope of winning it.[9]

Conditions such as Wickersham described were evidence of negative evaluation by a society which was opposed to the public education then emerging from the founding days of the early 1820's and 1830's.

There is this difference, however, between Wickersham's Pennsylvania past and America's present: administration then was only one step out of the teacher's role in the one-room school. It was a personalized function, completely new and strange to society. Those who supported the institution of public education with courage and fortitude saw the institution as an instrument for social, economic, vocational, and political change. It was a bootstrap motivation.

While these purposes are still with us in the 1960's, they are immeasurably augmented by a new society created *from* and *by* the public schools which were originally unwanted by so many. A new generation of citizens is demanding an even better educational program than they had in their childhood. This has happened because growing numbers of educated and still-growing Americans expect the schools of today to provide learning experiences for children who must cope with an onrushing present and face an awesome and unknown future.

In a world that harbors growing numbers of people who are grasping for new knowledge and skills and reaching for higher ideals, the demands on all institutions that have responsibility for education and on the leaders in these institutions are unprecedented. Faith that reason and understanding will, in the end, subordinate and control coercive force and enable mankind to live with dignity and in peace moves people in all walks of life to greater educational effort. Mediocrity in any aspect of the educational program can neither be tolerated nor afforded. There is

---

[9] Pennsylvania State Department of Public Instruction. *100 Years of Free Public Schools in Pennsylvania, 1834-1934.* Harrisburg: the Department, 1934. p. 60.

increasing determination to reach higher standards and to provide the best possible educational opportunities for children, youth, and adults with all their varying interests and abilities. This is the goal the people strive to reach; this is the challenge to school administration. It is an awesome but exciting call to American education.

# Name Index

# Subject Index